An Iowa Soldier Writes Home

January 31, 2015

To my friend + colleague:
    Irwin Block

In memory of our days together
on the Pitts-Lee Case 1960's + 1970's

Best wishes -
    Phil Hubbard

An Iowa Soldier Writes Home

*The Civil War Letters of Union Private
Daniel J. Parvin*

Edited with commentary by

Phillip A. Hubbart

CAROLINA ACADEMIC PRESS
Durham, North Carolina

Library of Congress Cataloging-in-Publication Data

Parvin, Daniel J. (Daniel James), 1826-1880.
  An Iowa soldier writes home : the Civil War letters of Union Private Daniel J.
Parvin / edited with commentary by Phillip A. Hubbart.
      p. cm.
  Includes bibliographical references.
  ISBN 978-1-59460-978-7 (alk. paper)
  1. Parvin, Daniel J. (Daniel James), 1826-1880--Correspondence. 2. United
States. Army. Iowa Infantry Regiment, 11th (1861-1865) 3. United States--
History--Civil War, 1861-1865--Personal narratives. 4. Iowa--History--Civil
War, 1861-1865--Personal narratives. 5. Soldiers--Iowa--Correspondence. 6.
Muscatine (Iowa)--Biography. I. Hubbart, Phillip A. II. Title.
  E507.511th .P37 2011
  973.7'8--dc22

                    2011002478

CAROLINA ACADEMIC PRESS
700 Kent Street
Durham, North Carolina 27701
Telephone (919) 489-7486
Fax (919) 493-5668
www.cap-press.com

In loving memory of my father and mother
Donald and Esther Hubbart

The Civil War's domestic impact was so extensive and varied that it almost defies description. Total casualties on both sides (360,000 Union, 258,000 Confederate) equal the number lost in all other American wars combined.

The percentage of the eligible population mobilized (50% in the North, 75% in the South) remains unsurpassed in Western military history.

The nearly four million African American slaves liberated by the war represent a process of emancipation unequaled in the Western Hemisphere in scope and degree of governmental coerciveness.

James Brewer Stewart
Prof. of History, Macalester College, St. Paul, Minn.

The Oxford Companion to American History 132 (2001)

Contents

Illustrations

Preface

This book is an edited collection of 117 letters that a Union soldier, Daniel J. Parvin, wrote home to his wife and family in Muscatine, Iowa, during the American Civil War (1861–65). Parvin went in as a private and came out as a corporal—so that these letters are a dog soldier's view of the war.

Despite run-on sentences, some misspellings and lack of paragraphing that had to be corrected in the editing process, Daniel J. Parvin emerges from these letters as a perceptive writer. He narrates relevant events with a keen eye for critical detail, particularly in his vivid and dramatic accounts of the battles he was in—the Battle of Shiloh [where he narrowly escaped death], the Siege of Vicksburg [where he served in a reserve capacity] and the Atlanta campaign [where he was seriously wounded and almost died]. He employs the same attention to detail in his descriptions of day-to-day camp life.

Parvin was also a passionate and opinionated man. He expresses his views in colorful language on the people, events and politics of his day—including his views on Lincoln, Grant, McClellan, the Emancipation Proclamation, Black Union regiments, southern sympathizers in the North, the Union and Confederate causes, rebel soldiers, and so on. And he often pours out his heart on the painful loneliness he felt away from home, and on the deep love he had for his family and country.

What is remarkable, however, about Parvin the man is that he can, on the one hand, fight so fiercely and with such loyalty for the Union cause, and yet, on the other hand, express his utter disdain for war and the soldiering life—as well as [at times] conceding an admiration and even a sympathy for the Confederate soldier. He is a complex, sensitive and intelligent man whom [I hope] the reader will soon come to like and admire. [I am indebted to my friend Dennis Dalton for this insight into Parvin's character.]

These letters are owned by, and are on display at, the Muscatine Art Center, in Muscatine, Iowa, Parvin's hometown. In 1977, Esther Hubbart, the great-granddaughter of Daniel J. Parvin, donated these letters to the Center so that they may be preserved for future generations. The Center, in turn, has graciously allowed this historic correspondence to be published in this volume—portions of which have been selected for inclusion therein.

My name is Phillip A. Hubbart. I am the great-great-grandson of Daniel J. Parvin. I am also the son of Esther Hubbart, and the editor of this book. I am not, however, a professional historian. I am a retired Florida state court appellate judge with a keen interest in my country's history—much like, I hope, the reader of this work.

This is a reader-friendly book. Whereas most other Civil War letter collections present each letter in chronological order, this book extracts portions of the letters and organizes them around certain stated themes. These themes represent subjects that, in the editor's view, readers most want to know about in the average soldier's life.

The reader can review the table of contents, select portions of the book that seem the most interesting, and read those portions without having to plow through the entire book. The reader can then pick up the book at a later time to read other subjects of interest. For the many readers out there with busy lives, this is no small advantage.

Yet this method does not sacrifice depth. To the contrary, this approach allows the reader to get a focused view of common experiences and contemporary people in a single chapter or section, that would otherwise have been scattered throughout the entire letters if a chronological approach were used. Moreover, I have used the research of respected historians and original sources in my commentary, to place Parvin's account within the context of his time and place.

Here is how the book is organized.

- **Introduction.** Chapter 1, among other things, covers a chronological breakdown [with maps] of Parvin's participation in the Civil War (1861–65)—so that the reader can place each letter in context. [Also, see the timeline of Parvin's Civil War service pages 157–61, infra.]
- **Military Engagements.** Chapter 2 deals with all of the letters that mention the military engagements in which Parvin was either involved or was near. Also included are letters dealing with Parvin's miraculous recovery from his near-fatal wounds suffered during the Atlanta campaign.
- **Opinions.** Chapter 3 deals with Parvin's often emphatic, even damning opinions of contemporary persons and events. These opinions were totally uncensored by his superiors.
- **Camp Life.** Chapter 4 deals with Parvin's experience with everyday camp life during his entire army service; e.g., writing and receiving letters, camp sickness and medical services, army food, army pay, army discipline, guard duty, picket duty, camp assignments, and so on.

- **Miscellaneous.** Chapter 5 is a catch-all chapter dealing with a series of striking subjects: Parvin's re-enlistment in the army in 1864, his contemplated enlistment in navy gunboat service, foraging the southern countryside, furloughs, travel experiences, a soldier's flights of fancy, and so on.

From these selections, I hope the reader can better understand the upheaval and tragedy of the Civil War by viewing it through the eyes of this forgotten foot soldier. Learned scholars have written sweeping accounts of the Civil War told largely from the perspective of political and military leaders. But how did an average soldier like Parvin experience it? This book tries to answer that question.

Acknowledgments

A number of people were of great help to me in putting this book together. Without them, the book would never have been completed as fast as it was—or with anything resembling its present quality.

First and foremost, I thank my sister-in-law Janice Nolin of Huntsville, Alabama, for the enormous amount of time and effort she put into this project. With her inquiring mind and her expert familiarity with Internet sources, she extensively researched both the genealogy of the Parvin family, and the history of Daniel J. Parvin's Iowa regiment. Time and again, she unraveled difficult family and military puzzles that baffled me. She also located an outstanding historical work on Parvin's regiment that I have used throughout this work—and prepared, as well, a valuable family tree for the book. I cannot thank her enough.

Deidre Pearson, formerly of the Muscatine Art Center, expertly transcribed Parvin's handwritten letters and e-mailed her transcriptions to me so that I could insert relevant portions of them into the book, which I was writing on my computer. She saved me a year or more of having to do the same laborious task from the xeroxed copies of the letters that I have—some of which are most difficult to read. She was also kind enough to photograph the tombstones of Daniel and Sarah Parvin at the Greenwood Cemetery in Muscatine, Iowa, that are included in this book. I am most indebted to her. Moreover, my friend Robert Stewart was most helpful in transcribing many of the letters that were quite difficult to read, for which I am most grateful.

Virginia Cooper, the registrar of the Muscatine Art Center, has been most generous in helping me coordinate this book with the informative exhibit of the Parvin letters at the Art Center that is scheduled to begin in the summer of 2011 on the 150th anniversary of the start of the Civil War. In the process of this happy cooperation, I was able to settle on the basic organization of this book. She also was kind enough to read the first draft of the book and offer helpful suggestions. Many, many thanks to her.

Tim Colton, the Production & Design Editor at Carolina Academic Press, secured and placed the Civil War maps that appear in the book. He also suggested that I visit the Library of Congress website to obtain appropriate Civil War photos for the book—all of which are in the public domain. I did so and the fine collection of Civil War photos that appear in the book are from that collection. I am most indebted to him.

I would like to thank Keith Sipe, the publisher at Carolina Academic Press [CAP], and the CAP Editorial Board, for agreeing to publish a book that is somewhat outside the scope of works that CAP ordinarily publishes. I am most appreciative. My thanks also go to Linda Lacy and Zoë Oakes, the Executive Editor and Acquisitions Assistant, respectively, at CAP for all their encouragement and help in this project. Moreover, Kelly Miller, the Production & Media Designer at CAP, designed the cover for the book, and inserted the photos and illustrations that appear therein—for which I am most grateful.

My aunt, Doris Rolfe, of Chandler, Arizona, has been most helpful in securing some of the family background for this book. Her late husband [and my uncle], Bob Rolfe, had a great interest in the Parvin letters, and, with his marvelous memory, was the repository of much of the genealogy of our family. Many thanks to my Aunt Doris and my Uncle Bob.

My many friends, too numerous to mention, showed great interest in this project and gave me a good deal of encouragement. Gerald Wetherington, Dennis Dalton, Pat Kruppa, Chuck Edelstein and Diane Thurston, in particular, were kind enough to read the text and give me their impressions. In addition, Dennis Dalton and Pat Kruppa did some useful proofreading work and offered valuable insights into Parvin's character. Also Aristides Millas, an accomplished architect, sketched out a partial Parvin family tree for me that was quite helpful in the ultimate product that appears in the book. I thank them all.

My deceased father and mother [Donald and Esther Hubbart] have been my inspiration for compiling and editing the letters for this book. Both were fascinated with these letters and read them with great care. My mother inherited the letters through the family and donated them to the Muscatine Art Center, Muscatine, Iowa—Daniel J. Parvin's hometown—so that they could be preserved for future generations. I cherish their memory.

My devoted wife Martha Hubbart expertly proofread the text, came up with the title for the book, and offered valuable suggestions for improving the work. She also took two excellent photographs that appear in this book. I cannot possibly put into words how much she has meant to me in the nearly 50 years of our treasured marriage.

Finally, I thank my great-great-grandfather Daniel J. Parvin for his lively writing, his perceptive observations, his passionate honesty—and, most of all, for the sacrifices he made for our country. Without him, there would be no book. With him, we experience in part the turbulent Civil War times in which he lived.

List of Abbreviations

Books

B. Catton	Bruce Catton, *The Civil War* (Houghton Mifflin Co.) (paperback ed.) (1988)
D.J. Eicher	Daniel J. Eicher, *The Longest Night: A Military History of the Civil War* (Simon & Schuster Paperbacks) (2001)
Encyclo. of Civil War	*Encyclopedia of the American Civil War: A Political, Social, and Military History* (W.W. Norton & Co.) (David S. Heidler & Jeanne T. Heildler eds) (2000)
B. Gue	Benjamin F. Gue, *History of Iowa From the Earliest Times to the Beginning of the Twentieth Century*, Vol. IV Iowa Biography (The Century History Co., New York) (1903)
W. Groom	Winston Groom, *Vicksburg 1863* (Vintage Civil War Library, Vintage Books, Div. of Random House, Inc.) (paperback ed.) (2009)
J.M. McPherson	James M. McPherson, *Battle Cry of Freedom* (Oxford Univ. Press) (1988)
J.E. Morcombe	Joseph E. Morcombe, *The Life and Labors of Theodore Sutton Parvin A.M. LL.D.* (Allen Printing Co., Clinton, Ia.) (1908)
Hist. Muscatine County	*History of Muscatine County Iowa From the Earliest Settlements to the Present Time*, Vol. I (S.J. Clarke Publishing Co., Chicago) (Irving B. Richman, supervising ed.) (1911)

Roster & Record, Hist. Skch.   *Roster and Record of Iowa Soldiers in the War of the Rebellion, Vol. II, 9th–16th Regiments— Infantry, "Historical Sketch Eleventh Regiment Iowa Volunteer Infantry"* (Des Moines, Ia.; Emory H. English, State Printer; E.D. Chassell, State Binder) (1908)

Roster & Record, 11th Reg.   *Roster and Record of Iowa Soldiers in the War of the Rebellion, Vol. II, 9th–16th Regiments— Infantry, "Eleventh Regiment Iowa Volunteer Infantry"* (Des Moines, Ia.; Emory H. English, State Printer; E.D. Chassell, State Binder (1908)

J.P. Walton   Josiah Proctor Walton, *Pioneer Papers: comprising a collection of early events of Bloomington, Iowa, now Muscatine, and its surroundings, being a short history of the business men, the schools, the churches and the early politics of the pioneers* (paperback) (originally published in Muscatine in 1899) (Nabu Press, August 31, 2010)

Web Sites

C.W. Soldrs. & Sailrs.   Civil War Soldiers and Sailors Website, National Park Service [n.ps.gov/cwss/soldiers.cfm]

Greenwood Cemetery Records   Greenwood Cemetery Records, Muscatine, Iowa, Ancestry.com

Ia.Gn.Wb.Prj.   Iowa Gen Web Project [iagenweb.org]

Register of Old Settlers   Muscatine County, Iowa, Register of Old Settlers, Book One, Iowa Gen Web Project [iagenweb.org]

An Iowa Soldier Writes Home

"If I fall in battle, my last thoughts will be on those that I left behind at home."

"I often think of home and the dear ones to me that I left behind. And I wish that the time may soon come when I can be there with them, and our country at peace. I think then that I could be happy."

—Pvt. Daniel J. Parvin, Eleventh Iowa Regiment, Company H, February 3, 1862 & March 8, 1863

Chapter 1

Introduction

This introductory chapter covers an overview of Daniel J. Parvin's immediate family, a chronological breakdown of Parvin's army service in the Civil War (1861–65), a genealogy of the Parvin letters, and finally an explanation of how the Parvin letters have been edited.

Section 1. An Overview of Parvin's Immediate Family

First, a brief look at Parvin's immediate family.[1] Daniel James Parvin [great-great-grandfather of this book's editor] was born August 12, 1826, in Hamilton County, Ohio [Cincinnati],[2] to William Parvin (1797–1882) and Hannah Wescott (1797–1882).[3] He was one of eight children born of this marriage.[4] The family moved to what later became known as Muscatine, Iowa, in 1839,[5] when Iowa was still a territory [Iowa was not admitted to the Union until 1846]. On July 1, 1848, William Parvin purchased from the U.S. General Land Office

---

1. By immediate family, we mean Parvin's mother and father, several of his siblings, his nephew, his two wives and his three children. No effort has been made, however, to track down the large number of other Parvin family members and in-laws—many of whom Parvin corresponded with during his army service. Parvin often names these relatives in his letters, and the reader's indulgence is requested when we do not always identify the relative with more particularity. A genealogical study of the entire Parvin family is simply beyond the scope of this work.

2. Greenwood Cemetery Records ["Daniel J. Parvin" search]; Register of Old Settlers at 92.

3. Register of Old Settlers at 130; Greenwood Cemetery Records ["William Parvin" search].

4. Register of Old Settlers at 130.

5. Register of Old Settlers at 130. An early biography of Theodore S. Parvin [a prominent Iowa pioneer and first cousin of Daniel J. Parvin] describes the arrival of William Parvin and family in Bloomington [later Muscatine], Iowa, on March 29, 1839. J.E. Morcombe at 108.

40 acres of land where the family lived in a log cabin—the same residence where William and his wife Hannah lived at the time of their respective deaths in 1882.[6] William served in a number of public offices in Muscatine during his lifetime, including county coroner—as well as city treasurer, collector and marshal.[7]

As the letters reveal, William's son Daniel J. Parvin was a bitter political opponent of the Democratic Party in the 1860s, and a supporter of Republican political candidates, including Abraham Lincoln.[8] William Parvin, on the other hand, was a life-long Democrat[9] whose political convictions were so strong that he refused to attend the wedding of one of his daughters, Lydia, to J.P. Freeman because Freeman was an abolitionist, and the wedding of another daughter, Elizabeth, to Alfred Purcell because Purcell was a Whig. William, in fact, left town to go hunting during both weddings.[10] The letters, however, do not reveal any political animosity between William and his son Daniel.[11]

In 1845, Daniel J. Parvin began to learn the cabinetmaking business with his brother-in-law J.P. Freeman in Muscatine, Iowa.[12] At the time, the town was named Bloomington, but in 1849 was renamed Muscatine; Parvin was one of the signatories to the petition seeking this name change.[13] In 1852, Parvin moved to California to seek his fortune and remained there until 1858; he then moved back to Muscatine, Iowa, resumed his cabinetmaking business

---

6. U.S. General Land Office Records 1796–1907, Ancestry.com ["William Parvin" search]; Register of Old Settlers at 130.

7. Register of Old Settlers at 130.

8. See generally the letters collected at Chapter 3, Sections 1d & 2, infra.

9. One historical authority states that William Parvin "took an active interest in politics and was a Democrat of the true Jeffersonian type." Register of Old Settlers at 130. Less charitably, however, he has also been referred to as an "an old 'moss-backed democrat.'" J.P. Walton at 313.

10. J.P. Walton at 313; Ia.Gen.Wb.Prj. [Muscatine County] Muscatine County Iowa Early Marriage Records 1837–1845 ["Joseph Freeman" search] ["Alfred Purcell" search].

11. There is, however, one cryptic reference in the letters in which Parvin declines to answer a portion of one of his father's letters relating to politics. This reference may indicate that political subjects were best left alone between them.

As regards your letter [his Father's] that relates to the abolition war and the change in politics, I shall not answer. [June 26, 1862: Corinth, Miss.]

12. Register of Old Settlers at 92; Ia.Gen.Wb.Prj. [Muscatine County] Muscatine County Iowa Early Marriage Records 1837–1845 ["Joseph Freeman" search].

13. J.P. Walton at 66–67. The town's name was changed from Bloomington to Muscatine on June 7, 1849, because there were towns of the same name in several other states, resulting in frequent misdelivery of letters. Hist. Muscatine County 287 (1911).

Figure 1. Tombstone of Daniel J. Parvin,
Greenwood Cemetery, Muscatine, Iowa

Courtesy of Deidre Pearson.

and, except for his Civil War service [1861–65], remained in Muscatine for the rest of his life.[14] He died February 24, 1880, at the age of 53 of cancer of the mouth directly related to a near-fatal wound to his mouth and jaw that he sustained in the Atlanta campaign.[15] He is buried in Greenwood Cemetery, Muscatine, Iowa.[16] See Figure 1.

---

14. Register of Old Settlers at 92. The 1866 City Directory for Muscatine, Iowa, lists Daniel J. Parvin's carpenter shop at "Third ns 2e Cedar" [ns=north side; e=east]. The 1876–77 Muscatine County History and Directory lists Daniel J. Parvin's residence at "39 Cedar."

15. 1880 Federal Census, Muscatine County, Iowa, Schedule 5, "Persons Who Died During the Year Ending May 31, 1880" lists Daniel J. Parvin as having died in February 1880 of "cancer in mouth," "caused by shot wound in army." His exact date of death is found in the records of Greenwood Cemetery, Muscatine, Iowa, where he is buried. Muscatine County, Iowa, Register of Old Settlers, Book One 92 states that Parvin "never fully recovered" from a war wound to the mouth and jaw sustained in the Battle of Atlanta, which was "undoubtedly the cause of his death." His near-fatal war wound is described in his September 12, 1864, letter contained at Chapter 2, Sec. 5, infra.

16. Daniel J. Parvin's burial site at Greenwood Cemetery, Muscatine, Iowa is verified by both his tombstone there and the records at Greenwood Cemetery.

Parvin married twice. The first was to Sarah A. Hermen (1841–1866) on April 12, 1860.[17] All 117 Civil War letters are addressed to Sarah and the Parvin family. He had three children by this marriage: Fred Parvin (1860–65),[18] Charles M. Parvin (1864–1950),[19] and George W. Parvin (1865–1915).[20] The letters mention Fred and a second unnamed baby later named Charles.[21] Daniel and Sarah's marriage was cut short when Sarah died in 1866 at the age of 25. She is buried in Greenwood Cemetery, Muscatine, Iowa. See Figure 2.

Daniel's second marriage on March 15, 1868, was to Sophronia Selden (1825–1912)—two years after Sarah's death.[22] No children were born of this

---

17. Ia.Gen.Wb.Prj. [Muscatine County] Muscatine County Iowa Marriage Index 1846–1875["Daniel J. Parvin" search]; Greenwood Cemetery Records & Tombstone ["Sarah Parvin" search]. As an aside, however, Sarah is also listed as "Sarah A. Hening" [not Hermen] in the tribute to Daniel J. Parvin upon the latter's death. Register of Old Settlers at 92. She is further listed as "Sarah Ann Hennen"[not Hermen] in a secondary marriage record when her son Charles Parvin applied for a marriage license in Muscatine, Iowa, to marry Annie Old circa 1924. Iowa Marriages 1809–1992, familysearch.org/s/record ["Charles Mulford Parvin" search].

18. The birth and death dates for Fred Parvin are taken from his tombstone at Greenwood Cemetery, Muscatine, Iowa, where he is buried.

19. The birth and death dates for Charles Parvin are taken from State of California Death Index 1940–1997, Ancestry.com ["Charles Mulford Parvin"search]. Charles' wife Annie died on October 9, 1952, in Long Beach, California, according to her funeral services papers possessed by the editor's family.

Charles was a widower when he married Annie. He was previously married to Katie R. Goeser on May 16, 1888. Ia.Gen.Wb.Prj. [Muscatine County] Muscatine County Iowa Marriage Index 1851–1900 ["Charles M. Parvin" search]. Katie died in 1922 and is buried in Greenwood Cemetery, Muscatine Iowa. Greenwood Cemetery Records. So far as we are aware, there were no children born of this marriage.

20. The birth and death dates for George W. Parvin are taken from the records of Greenwood Cemetery, Muscatine, Iowa, where he is buried. His death date is further verified by the Muscatine County Genealogical Society Probate Documents Name Index 1900–1942 ["George W. Parvin" search], Ia.Gen.Web.Prj. [Muscatine County].

21. Daniel J. Parvin's letters concerning his two children, Fred and Charles, can be found at Chapter 5, Section 8b of this work.

22. The marriage date for Daniel and Sophronia is taken from the Muscatine County Iowa Marriage Index 1846–1875 ["Daniel J. Parvin" search] [Ia.Gen.Wb.Prj., Muscatine County] [Sophronia's surname listed as "Selden"]. The birth and death dates for Sophronia Parvin are taken from her tombstone at Greenwood Cemetery, as well as the Greenwood Cemetery Records.

Sophronia's marriage to Daniel was her second. She was previously married to Harris Selden and had a son by that marriage, James Selden. Sophronia's maiden name was Allyn. State of Texas Bureau of Vital Statistics, Death Certificate for James Selden (Dec. 21, 1925); 1880 Federal Census, Muscatine, Iowa "Sophronia Parvin" ["Selden" inaccurately spelled "Seldin"].

Figure 2. Tombstone of Sarah Parvin, Greenwood Cemetery, Muscatine, Iowa

Courtesy of Deidre Pearson.

marriage. Upon Daniel's death, Sophronia received a pension as a Union Civil War widow.[23] To more fully understand Daniel's relationship to the many members of his immediate and extended family, see Figure 3 for a Parvin Partial Family Tree.

Unfortunately, we have no surviving photograph of Daniel J. Parvin. But see Figure 4 for a photograph of Charles Parvin [Daniel J. Parvin's son], and Charles' wife Annie, taken in December 1932, in Muscatine, Iowa.

Section 2. Daniel J. Parvin's Civil War Service

We turn now to Parvin's long service with his Iowa regiment in the Civil War. This review is most important in placing in proper context the letters that are extracted in the chapters that follow.

---

23. Civil War Pension Index: General Index to Pension Files. Ancestry.com ["Daniel J. Parvin" search]. The 1883 Muscatine County Military Pension Roll states that Sophronia Parvin was receiving an $8.00-a-month pension as a widow under the claim no. 196.213, beginning June 1882. Muscatine County Iowa 1883 Military Pension Index ["Sophronia Parvin"] [rootsweb.ancestry.com/~iamusca2/1883pension.htm.]

Figure 3. Parvin Partial Family Tree. Courtesy of Janice Nolin.

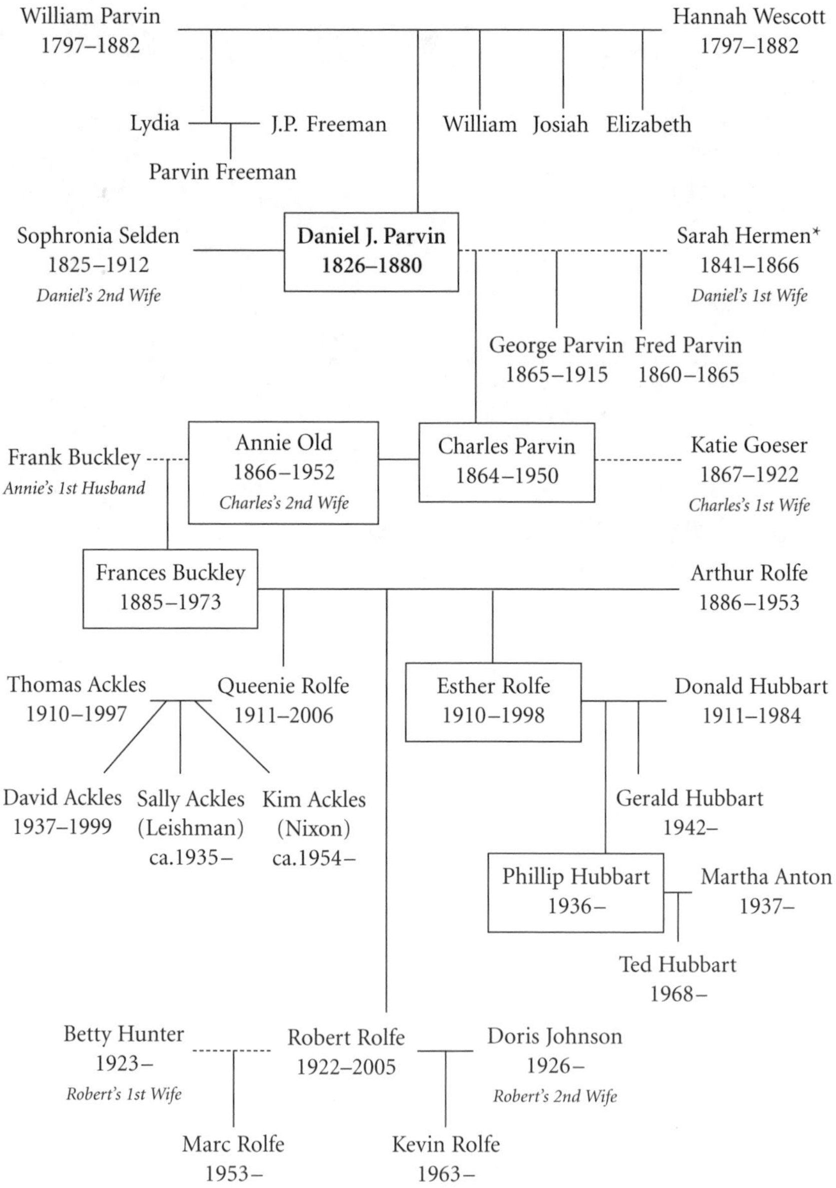

William Parvin
1797–1882

Hannah Wescott
1797–1882

Lydia — J.P. Freeman

William Josiah Elizabeth

Parvin Freeman

Sophronia Selden
1825–1912
Daniel's 2nd Wife

**Daniel J. Parvin
1826–1880**

Sarah Hermen*
1841–1866
Daniel's 1st Wife

George Parvin
1865–1915

Fred Parvin
1860–1865

Frank Buckley
Annie's 1st Husband

Annie Old
1866–1952
Charles's 2nd Wife

Charles Parvin
1864–1950

Katie Goeser
1867–1922
Charles's 1st Wife

Frances Buckley
1885–1973

Arthur Rolfe
1886–1953

Thomas Ackles
1910–1997

Queenie Rolfe
1911–2006

Esther Rolfe
1910–1998

Donald Hubbart
1911–1984

David Ackles
1937–1999

Sally Ackles
(Leishman)
ca.1935–

Kim Ackles
(Nixon)
ca.1954–

Gerald Hubbart
1942–

Phillip Hubbart
1936–

Martha Anton
1937–

Ted Hubbart
1968–

Betty Hunter
1923–
Robert's 1st Wife

Robert Rolfe
1922–2005

Doris Johnson
1926–
Robert's 2nd Wife

Marc Rolfe
1953–

Kevin Rolfe
1963–

Note: Names shown inside the boxes trace the transmittal of Daniel J. Parvin's letters from one generation to the next.

* *Variant spellings of Sarah Hermen's last name in historical sources appear as Henning or Hennen.*

Figure 4. Charles Parvin and Annie Parvin, 1932

Courtesy of the Musser Public Library, Oscar Grossheim Collection, Muscatine, Iowa.

On September 21, 1861, Daniel J. Parvin enlisted as a private in the Union Army at the age of 35 in Muscatine, Iowa. He was much older than his fellow recruits and was attached to the Eleventh Iowa Regiment, Company H, for his entire Civil War service.[24]

Col. Abraham M. Hare and Lt. Col. William Hall were the top commissioned officers for the Eleventh Iowa Regiment. Captain Benjamin Beach, First Lt. George D. Magoon and Second Lt. George R. White were the commanding line officers for Company H.[25]

Parvin re-enlisted as a veteran on January 1, 1864.[26] On February 25, 1865, he was discharged as a corporal after suffering gruesome war wounds sustained

24. The information in this paragraph is taken from Muscatine County, Iowa Civil War Soldiers Records, "Daniel J. Parvin," Ancestry.com.

25. The information in this paragraph is taken from Roster & Record, 11th Reg. 284, 286.

26. Roster & Record, 11th Reg. at 372.

on August 20, 1864, during the Atlanta campaign.[27] As revealed by the letters, most of his lower jaw and almost all his teeth were shot off.[28]

Parvin fought as well in the Battle of Shiloh [the first great engagement of the Civil War] and narrowly escaped death while soldiers all around him were shot, wounded and killed. He was also involved in the Siege of Vicksburg which fell July 4, 1863—and participated in other skirmishes in Mississippi and Tennessee. He served under General Ulysses S. Grant at Shiloh and Vicksburg, and under General William T. Sherman at Atlanta.

What follows is a brief chronological description of his deployment during the Civil War (1861–65).[29] See also a timeline of Parvin's Civil War service at pages 157–61 of this book.

Initial Training and Deployment Period: Iowa and Missouri [September 1861–February 1862]

Following his enlistment in September, 1861, Parvin was sent to Camp McClellan in Davenport, Iowa, where his regiment was organized and clothing and supplies issued. Davenport is located on the Mississippi River about 20 miles upstream from Muscatine.

Between September 14 and October 19, 1861, all ten companies of the Eleventh Iowa Regiment, amounting to 922 soldiers at that time, were mustered into service by Captain Alexander Chambers of the U.S. Army. Parvin remained at Camp McClellan through the middle of November.

On November 16, 1861, Parvin was sent by steamship ["the Jennie Whipple"] down the Mississippi River to a very large army training facility, Benton Barracks, located just outside St. Louis, Missouri. While there, he received ad-

---

27. Parvin's discharge date as a corporal due to war wounds is found at U.S. Civil War Soldiers 1861–65, "Daniel J. Parvin," and Iowa Civil War Soldier Burial Records, "Daniel J. Parvin," Ancestry.com. Parvin most likely was promoted from private to corporal after he was wounded, as the letters do not reveal any such promotion while he was in active service. Parvin's war wound at the Atlanta campaign and the date he was hit are found at Roster & Record, 11th Reg. at 372.

28. The account of how Parvin was wounded in the Atlanta campaign and his medical treatment thereafter is found in his September 12, 1864, letter written from an army hospital in Marietta, Georgia, and is included in Chapter 2, Section 5, of this work.

29. The details concerning Parvin's deployment in the Civil War with the Eleventh Iowa Regiment are taken from (1) the Parvin letters themselves; (2) Roster & Record, Hist.Skch. at 275–83, and Roster & Record, 11th Reg. at 284, 337; and (3) Hist. Muscatine County at 137–41.

ditional supplies and drilled with his regiment in preparation for battle. He remained there for about three weeks.

On December 9, 1861, he was deployed by train to two locations directly west of St. Louis, along the Missouri River, to Jefferson City and California, Missouri. He remained there through February 1862.

Near the middle of December 1861, he engaged in a scouting expedition to nearby Boonville, Missouri, on the Missouri River, and rounded up some Confederate prisoners, but without firing any shots. He was also aware of other scouting expeditions in the immediate area.

For the reader's convenience, see Figure 5 for a map of Iowa and Missouri showing Parvin's enlistment and training sites in Davenport, Iowa, and St. Louis, Missouri—and his initial deployment into the interior of Missouri.

Battle of Shiloh: Pittsburg Landing, Tennessee [April 6–7, 1862]

On March 12, 1862, Parvin was transported with his regiment to Pittsburg Landing, Tennessee, to engage in the historic Battle of Shiloh [April 6–7, 1862], the first major engagement of the Civil War.

To get there, Parvin traveled by steamboat south from St. Louis on the Mississippi River to the Ohio River, then east on the Ohio River for a short distance to the Tennessee River, and then south on the Tennessee River to the battle site at Pittsburg Landing, Tennessee. This location is about 20 miles north of Corinth, Mississippi, the Confederate headquarters for this battle and a major rail center at the time. The battle was named after Shiloh Church, a small rustic house of worship in the immediate area.

Parvin's regiment was assigned to the First Brigade of the First Division of the Army of the Tennessee in this battle. General John A. McClernand was in command of this division; Colonel A.M. Hare of the Eleventh Iowa Regiment was in command of this brigade. The Eleventh Iowa Regiment, however, was detached from the brigade early in the battle, and was commanded by Colonel William Hall.

In this historic conflict, Parvin was in the thick of the action with men all around him hit, wounded and killed; miraculously, he survived virtually unscathed. Although there were horrific losses on both sides, the Union forces eventually prevailed and the Confederates were forced to withdraw to Corinth, Mississippi. General Albert Johnston, the commanding Confederate general in the battle, was killed in action.

Figure 5. Parvin's Enlistment/Training Sites and
Initial Deployment (1861–62)

For the reader's convenience, see Figure 6 for a map of Parvin's deployment from Missouri to the Battle of Shiloh at Pittsburg Landing, Tennessee.

Corinth, Mississippi Campaign and Aftermath
[April 1862–January 1863]

On April 27, 1862, after the Shiloh Battle, Parvin's regiment was assigned to a brigade consisting of the Eleventh, Thirteenth, Fifteenth and Sixteenth Regiments of Iowa Infantry under the command of Colonel M.M. Crocker of the Thirteenth Regiment. From that date forward, these regiments served together to the end of the war and were known as Crocker's Brigade—although they were commanded at times by officers other than Colonel Crocker.

General Henry Halleck took command of the Union forces in the area after Shiloh, regrouped at Pittsburg Landing, and slowly advanced on Corinth, Mississippi, over the next three weeks, covering but 20 miles. On June 5, 1862, when Parvin's regiment finally arrived in Corinth, the Confederates had already successfully evacuated the town. During this period, there were no skirmishes in which Parvin participated.

For the next five months, Parvin and his regiment were camped in and around Corinth, Mississippi. During this time, Parvin was sent out to engage in two skirmishes with the Confederates. One was around Bolivar, Tennessee, during which he received a minor wound to his ear. The other was around Ripley, Mississippi, in which his company and others chased the Confederates, who were in full retreat.

In early November 1862, Parvin and his regiment left Corinth permanently and marched a short distance to Grand Junction, Tennessee [just over the Mississippi state line], then south some 50 miles to Abbeyville and Oxford, Mississippi. In these expeditions, they were in search of Confederate forces but found none. Finally, they left the area and marched northwest to Memphis, Tennessee, on the Mississippi River, arriving there in early January 1863.

For the reader's convenience, see Figure 7 depicting Parvin's deployment around Corinth, Mississippi, his skirmishes to Bolivar, Tennessee, and Ripley, Mississippi, and his eventual march to Memphis, Tennessee.

The Vicksburg Campaign and Aftermath
[February 1863–March 1864]

In late January 1863, Parvin and his regiment left Memphis and went south by steamboat down the Mississippi River to join Union forces in preparation for the eventual capture of Vicksburg, Mississippi. This city was a seemingly

Figure 6. Parvin's deployment from Missouri to the
Battle of Shiloh (1862)

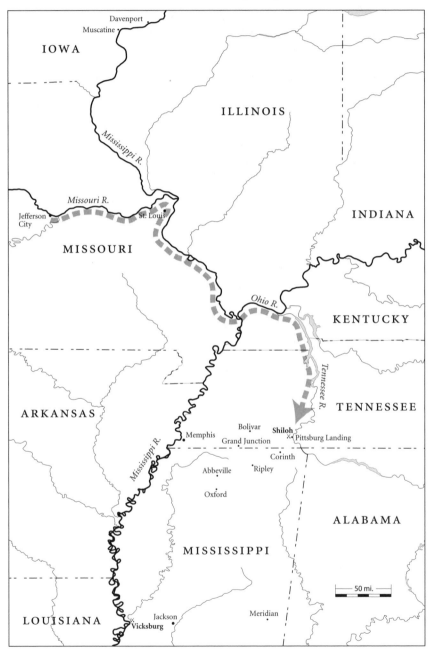

Figure 7. Parvin's Deployments Around Corinth, Mississippi and
March to Memphis, Tennessee (1862–63)

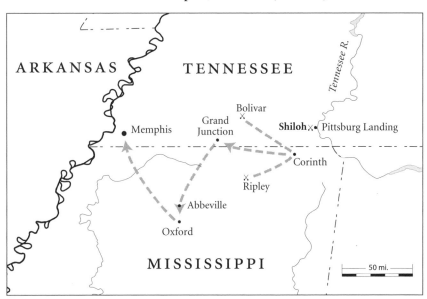

impenetrable Confederate stronghold located on a steep bluff overlooking the
Mississippi River, a number of miles downstream from Memphis.

Parvin was thereafter encamped at a number of locations in and around
the Vicksburg area and was on alert for any action if required. There was fighting all around him, but Parvin participated in no actual skirmishes. After the
fall of Vicksburg, Parvin was encamped for some eight months in the immediate area and did garrison duty to protect the city against rebel attacks.

Although not clear from the letters, Parvin was apparently wounded in some
unknown skirmish in early August 1863, was given a short furlough home to
Muscatine—and returned by steamboat to Vicksburg in early September. The
letters reveal no details concerning the nature of Parvin's wound, how he in-
curred it, or the details of the furlough.

Later, in February 1864, Parvin and his brigade participated in a skirmish
directly east of Vicksburg in which the Confederates were driven past Meridian, Mississippi, near the Alabama border. General William T. Sherman commanded this expedition.

For the reader's convenience, see Figure 8 for a map of Tennessee and Mississippi depicting Parvin's deployment in the Vicksburg campaign and his in-
volvement in the later expedition to Meridian, Mississippi.

Figure 8. Parvin's Deployment from Memphis, Tennessee to the
Vicksburg Campaign and Its Aftermath (1863–64)

The Atlanta Campaign and Aftermath
[May–October 1864]

On January 1, 1864, Parvin and a majority of the men in his regiment re-enlisted as veterans for another three-year term. As a reward for so doing, in early
March 1864, Parvin and all those who had re-enlisted were given a thirty-day

furlough. They were transported from Vicksburg via the steamboat "Continental" to Davenport, Iowa, following which Parvin returned home to Muscatine.

On April 22, 1864, Parvin and his fellow re-enlisted veterans [together with some fresh recruits] ended their furlough and re-assembled at Davenport, Iowa. They were then transported by steamboat south on the Mississippi River, and then east on the Ohio River to Cairo, Illinois, where they remained for a few days. Thereafter, they were transported by steamboat east on the Ohio River, then south on the Tennessee River to Clifton, Tennessee, a little north of Pittsburgh Landing, Tennessee, where they remained for about ten days.

From that point forward, Parvin marched with his brigade for over 300 miles through Huntsville, Alabama, and beyond, where he participated in the historic Atlanta campaign. Parvin saw some fierce fighting in a number of battles during this long campaign, which he describes in great detail in his letters. Two of these furious battles were at Kennesaw Mountain and Nickajack Creek, Georgia, northwest of Atlanta, in late June and early July 1864.

On August 20, 1864, Parvin was seriously wounded outside Atlanta; most of his jaw and almost all his teeth were shot off. He was taken to a nearby field hospital where he was apparently left to die, as he was bleeding profusely. But he miraculously survived, and was transferred to an army hospital in Marietta, Georgia; on September 6, 1864, he writes his first letter from this hospital. Atlanta itself fell to Union troops on September 2, 1864.

Eventually, Parvin recovered from his wounds after a long period of recuperation, and was mustered out of the army as a corporal on February 25, 1865. He returned to Muscatine and lived out the balance of his life.

For the reader's convenience, see Figure 9 for a map depicting Parvin's deployment in the Atlanta Campaign (1864).

Total Casualties in the Eleventh Iowa Regiment

During the course of the Civil War, 1297 soldiers enlisted in Parvin's Eleventh Iowa Regiment. Of that number, 58 were killed in action, 234 were wounded [27 of whom later died], and 154 died of disease—for a total of 446 casualties, over a third of all the soldiers in the regiment.

Parvin was also one of 179 soldiers who were discharged for wounds, disease or other causes. And of the total enlistees, 42 soldiers were transferred elsewhere, and 111 soldiers were later buried in national cemeteries.[30]

---

30. The statistics in this paragraph and the prior one are taken from Roster & Record, Hist.Skch. at 283.

Figure 9. Parvin's Deployment in the Atlanta Campaign (1864)

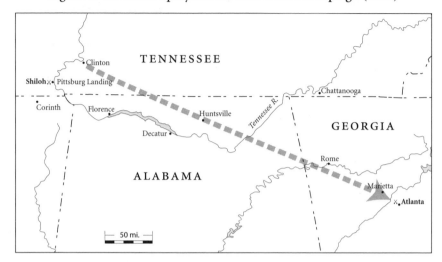

Section 3. Genealogy of the Parvin Letters

Next, a personal word on the genealogy of the Parvin letters. As the editor of these letters, my family relationship to this valuable correspondence has made this project particularly rewarding.

I am a retired Florida appellate court judge residing in Miami, Florida, where I have lived with my wife Martha for nearly 50 years. Our son Ted is a great-great-great grandson of Daniel J. Parvin. Ted, his wife Maritza, and their two children, Bradley and Allison, currently live outside Orlando, Florida.[31]

My mother, Esther Hubbart (1910–1998), inherited the Parvin letters through her grandfather, Charles Parvin (1864–1950)—the son of Daniel J. Parvin. Charles Parvin's wife was Annie Old Parvin (1866–1952).

From my childhood, I remember Charles and Annie Parvin [my great-grand parents] quite well. Annie Parvin was an attractive and vivacious woman.

---

31. As an aside, I have four living first cousins [on my mother's side of the family] who are also great-great-grandchildren of Daniel J. Parvin: Sally Leishman, Kim Nixon, and Marc and Kevin Rolfe. Sally and Kim are sisters and live in the Los Angles, California area. Marc and Kevin are stepbrothers; Marc lives in the Los Angles area; Kevin lives in Chandler, Arizona. I also had another cousin on the same side of the family, David Ackles, who has since passed away and was also a great-great-grandson of Daniel J. Parvin. David was the brother of Sally Leishman and Kim Nixon, and lived in the Los Angles area. Partial Family Tree at Figure 3, page 8, of this Chapter.

Charles Parvin, on the other hand, was a very quiet and sweet man, an agreeable contrast to his outspoken wife. I like to think that Daniel J. Parvin had many of his son's fine qualities—although the Parvin letters also reveal an angry side as well, perhaps befitting a brave and fierce soldier.

Charles and Annie Parvin lived in Muscatine, Iowa.[32] As I was growing up, some 20 miles away in Rock Island, Illinois, my immediate family would visit the Parvins from time to time. My father was Donald C. Hubbart (1911–1984), and my brother is Gerald D. Hubbart (1942–), currently a retired Florida state trial judge in Miami, Florida. Gerald, like myself, is also a great-great-grandson of Daniel J. Parvin. He is a military veteran like Parvin, having fought in the army with distinction as a second lieutenant in the Vietnam War.

Eventually Charles and Annie Parvin moved to Southern California to be close to Frances Rolfe—Annie Parvin's daughter by a previous marriage. In time, both Charles and Annie Parvin passed away in 1950 and 1952, respectively.[33]

In October 1977 Esther Hubbart [my mother] donated the Parvin letters to the Muscatine Art Center, Muscatine, Iowa—Daniel J. Parvin's home town—so that this valuable correspondence might be preserved for future generations. My brother Gerald and I were [and still are] in total agreement with this decision. The letters currently rest in the Muscatine Art Center for public viewing upon proper request. For easier reading, they have also been skillfully and laboriously transcribed by Deidre Pearson, formerly of the Center's staff.

As an aside, I have inherited from my mother a beautiful secretary that was made by Daniel J. Parvin sometime during his working years in Muscatine, Iowa. As previously noted, Parvin was a cabinetmaker by trade, and I am informed that he made this exquisite piece without using any nails. My will and my wife's will leaves this secretary to the Muscatine Art Center—and, accordingly, it may eventually be on display at the Art Center for public viewing. See Figure 10 for a photograph of Parvin's secretary.

---

32. The 1925 Iowa State Census Collection, Ancestry.com lists Charles Parvin as head of the household living in Muscatine, Iowa, with his wife Annie Old. The 1930 Federal Census for Muscatine, Iowa, [Ancestry.com], has the same listing.

33. Our family has funeral service papers for Annie Parvin that give her birth date as January 2, 1866, and her death date as October 9, 1952. She and her husband, Charles Parvin, resided in Long Beach, California at the time of their respective deaths. These dates are verified by the California Death Index 1940–1997, Ancestry.com ["Annie Parvin" search].

Figure 10. Secretary Built by Daniel J. Parvin

Courtesy of Martha Hubbart.

Section 4. Editing of the Parvin Letters

Finally, a brief note on how the Parvin letters have been edited.

- Each of the letters was originally written in one paragraph—no doubt to allow a maximum of news for the limited letter paper that Parvin had available. Consequently, the letters have been appropriately paragraphed.
- Run-on sentences in the original letters—and they abound—have been appropriately broken up with proper punctuation.
- Misspellings are frequent and have, for the most part, been corrected.
- Capital letters have been inserted when small letters were incorrectly employed—and vice-versa.
- Footnotes have been added at appropriate points to help explain relevant material in the letters.

Aside from these alterations to allow for easier reading, the letters [with Parvin's colloquialisms and sometimes improper grammar] are reproduced as they were originally written. This is done to give an honest and accurate picture of Parvin, the man and his times—and to avoid spoiling the style of a gifted writer.

For those readers who wish to view the letters in their unedited form, they are available for viewing upon proper request at the Muscatine Art Center in Muscatine, Iowa.

Chapter 2

Military Engagements

At the outset of his army service when he first arrived at Benton Barracks in St. Louis, Missouri, Parvin witnessed a tremendous amassing of troops and building of boats and rafts in preparation for army operations in the western theater of the Civil War. He wrote at the time:

> The army is preparing for something. There are now from forty to sixty thousand soldiers around St. Louis. And they are a-building boats and rafts in great numbers, and the soldiers are a-coming in here by the thousands every day. [Dec. 2, 1861: St. Louis, Mo.]

During his three and one half years of army service that followed, Parvin saw a great deal of action in the form of major battles, skirmishes and other military expeditions. In particular, he participated in the Battle of Shiloh, the Siege of Vicksburg and the Atlanta campaign. He also was aware of other nearby skirmishes and expeditions in which he was not involved. In chronological order, the following letters describe these often harrowing war experiences in great detail.

Section 1. Boonville, Missouri Expedition and Other Missions [December 1861–January 1862]

From St. Louis, Parvin was shipped by rail on December 9, 1861, to Jefferson City and later on December 23, 1861, to California, Missouri—both located on the Missouri River west of St. Louis.[1] While in Jefferson City, Parvin and his regiment were sent out on a nearby expedition to engage some Confederate militia units that were active in the area. The expedition consisted of a trip northwest on the Missouri River to Boonville, Missouri. Although no shots were fired when they got there, a number of Confederate prisoners were taken.

---

1. Roster & Record, Hist. Skch. at 275.

Parvin was also aware of other similar scouting expeditions in the area in which Confederate soldiers were taken prisoner. As an aside, when asked in a letter from home whether he had tried his gun yet, Parvin drily replied: "I have but I do not like it much. But it will do to shoot folks with." [Dec. 20, 1861: Jefferson City, Mo.]

In an earlier letter, Parvin states that "we expect to be sent out after Price and we hear he is near Jefferson, City, Mo." [Dec. 7, 1861: St. Louis, Mo.] No doubt he was referring to General Sterling Price, the commander of the pro-Southern militia in Missouri. Although a slave state, Missouri never seceded and remained in Union hands throughout the Civil War—after some early decisive Union victories. Nonetheless, pro-southern guerillas remained active in Missouri throughout the War.[2] It is therefore probable that Parvin and his company, as well as other companies, were sent out to engage some of General Price's militia.

Parvin describes the Boonville expedition in the following letter.

Dec. 19–20, 1861
Jefferson City, Mo.

Dear wife and relatives,

*** Dec. 20. *** Now for that expedition. We marched (that is the eleventh regiment) down to the river[3] and there was three steamboats and four companies of cavalry waiting for us. So we all went on board, and just at dark we started up the river and we ran nearly all night. And about daylight we landed at a little town by the name of Providence.[4] We heard that the rebels were in camp twelve hundred strong about ten miles back at some little town—I have forgotten the name. And so we marched back there but we found only a very few and they offered no resistance. So we took a few prisoners and marched back to the boats again.

We got back about nine o'clock Sunday night, and then we started up the river again. And the next morning at daylight we were in Boonville[5] and we laid there two or three hours and then we ran across the river.[6] The enemy were said to be collecting stores about fifteen

---

2. J.M. McPherson at 292–93.

3. This was undoubtedly the Missouri River, which flows directly past Jefferson City, Missouri.

4. This town has since died, but at the time was located northwest of Jefferson City on the Missouri River about halfway between Jefferson City and Boonville, Missouri.

5. Boonville is located a short distance northwest of Jefferson City on the Missouri River.

6. Parvin uses the terms "laid" and "ran" in their nautical sense. The word "lay" or "laid" is defined, inter alia, as "*Naut.* to take up a specified position, direction etc.: *to lay close to*

miles back from the river. So we started the cavalry and four companies of the eleventh, reserving the other six companies to guard the boats.

I was among the reserve and about eleven o'clock that night we were aroused from our slumbers by our officers and ordered to be ready to march immediately. The report was that the enemy were encamped sixty strong about five miles off. So we started in hopes of surprising them but when we got there, they had gone or else they had never been there. I could not find out which.

On the road some of the boys surrounded a house supposed to have an officer in it. And somehow one of our own men got separated from the rest and one of the boys mistook him for the man that they had been looking for and cried out here he goes, shoot him, and fired his gun at him. And at that another gun was fired at him, but neither one hit him but he was scared a little I guess.

When we got back to the boats, we found that the cavalry found and took one hundred and seventy-two kegs of powder of the best quality. And the next day or Wednesday we started down the river again. We started about noon and run that day until night and then we laid up until morning and then we came on down to Jefferson City. And here we are now but how long we will be here I cannot tell.
∗ ∗ ∗

I remain Yours forever   Danl. J. Parvin

———————

Parvin was aware of other similar expeditions in the area that also resulted in the capture of Confederate soldiers, as seen by the following letter.

California, Mo. [Moniteau County]
Jan. 28, 1862

Dear Wife and relatives

∗ ∗ ∗

Our scouting parties have been doing a little. We have taken some seventy-five or a hundred prisoners and nearly provisions enough to keep us. We have sent about twenty-five prisoners to St. Louis; the rest have

———————

the wind." Random House Webster's College Dictionary 768, def. no. 37 (Random House) (1995). The word "run" or "ran" is defined, inter alia, as "to sail before the wind." Random House Webster's College Dictionary at 1176, def. no. 32.

taken the oath.[7] And our scouts are out nearly every day. Some days they catch one or two of Price's men and other days they get nothing.
* * *

from one who loves you
Danl J. Parvin

Section 2. Battle of Shiloh: Pittsburg Landing, Tennessee [April 6–7, 1862]

After the bitter winter of 1861–62 in Missouri, Parvin and his regiment were shipped by rail and steamboat to Tennessee to participate in the Battle of Shiloh. Shiloh was the first major battle of the Civil War, and it was one of the bloodiest. In two days of fierce fighting [April 6–7, 1862], the Union casualties amounted to approximately 13,000, and the Confederate casualties approximately 10,500.[8] It took place at Pittsburgh Landing, Tennessee, next to the Tennessee River, about 20 miles northeast of Corinth, Mississippi, which was the Confederate headquarters for this battle. The battle is named after Shiloh Methodist Church, a rustic meeting house located on the field of battle. See Figure 11 for a reconstructed version of this small church as it currently stands.

Parvin's regiment was assigned to the First Brigade of the First Division of the Army of the Tennessee in this battle. General John A. McClernand was in command of this division; Colonel A.M. Hare of the Iowa Eleventh Regiment was in command of this brigade. From the first day of the battle, however, the Iowa Eleventh Regiment was detached from the First Brigade due to the pow-

---

7. Union and Confederate soldiers taken prisoner were sometimes paroled to return home upon their sworn promise not to rejoin their respective army—as opposed to being transferred to a prison camp. J.M. McPherson at 791–92. General Grant, in fact, gave such paroles to 30,000 captured Confederate soldiers after the fall of Vicksburg in July 1863. B. Catton at 141. But, for a variety of reasons, that policy changed by the end of 1863; captured soldiers were sent to prison camps and were no longer exchanged or paroled. J.M. McPherson at 792. Nonetheless, at the end of the war in April 1865, General Grant paroled all the Confederate soldiers who were captured at Appomattox. B. Catton at 260.

8. The exact Union casualties at Shiloh were: 1,754 killed, 8,408 wounded, and 2,885 missing; the exact Confederate casualties at Shiloh were: 1,728 killed, 8,012 wounded, and 959 missing. D.J. Eicher at 230. "The scale of the death at Shiloh, by far the largest battle fought in America to date, stunned the nation." Id. at 230. "Shiloh launched the country onto the floodtide of total war." J.M. McPherson at 414.

Figure 11. Shiloh Methodist Church

Courtesy of the editor.

erful thrust of the initial Confederate attack and fought as a regiment under the subordinate command of Colonel William Hall, who received orders from various superior officers in the field, including his commanding generals.[9]

During the first day of the battle, Parvin's regiment fought valiantly from 9:30 a.m. to 11 a.m. to hold back a concerted Confederate attack from the south just over the Corinth Road near Water Oaks Pond, until the regiment was forced to retreat north to a second position at Jones Field, about 100 yards in front of the regiment's camp. Of its 763 soldiers involved in this furious engagement, the Iowa Eleventh Regiment suffered 389 casualties. One officer and 33 men were killed; five officers [including Col. Hall] and 155 men were wounded; and 195 men were missing. Parvin was in the thick of this historic engagement, firing away at the Confederates throughout, while men all around him were hit, wounded and killed. Miraculously, he survived virtually unscathed. A monument has been erected to the Iowa Eleventh Regiment at the scene of this bloody battle at Shiloh National Military Park and is included herein as Figure 12.[10]

---

9. The information in this paragraph is taken from Roster & Record, Hist. Skch. at 276–79; and Hist. Muscatine County 138.

10. The information in this paragraph is taken from Shiloh Battlefield, Battlefield America, a Civil War Map Series, Trailhead Graphics, Inc. (2009); Roster & Record, Hist. Skch.

Figure 12. Monument to the Iowa Eleventh Regiment at the Shiloh
Battlefield Where Parvin Fought

Courtesy of Martha Hubbart.

In spite of the horrific losses suffered on both sides, the Union forces eventually prevailed. General Albert Johnston, the commanding Confederate general in this battle, was killed during the first day of the conflict.[11]

General Ulysses S. Grant was the commanding general of the Union forces at Shiloh. In the letters, Parvin flatly states that he lacked any confidence in Grant's leadership—probably because on the first day of the battle, Grant was caught by surprise and driven back almost to the Tennessee River, with considerable casualties.

On the second day, however, Grant's forces rallied with the help of 25,000 fresh troops led by General Don Carlos Buell, and drove the Confederates from the field of battle. The Confederates then retreated to their headquarters in Corinth, Mississippi, under the command of General P.G.T. Beauregard who

---

276–79; and a plaque on the aforesaid Iowa monument at Shiloh National Military Park.

As an aside, it was a strange feeling for the editor of this book when he stood on the ground of this bloody encounter during a recent visit to the Shiloh Battlefield, where his great-great-grandfather Daniel J. Parvin had fought almost 150 years ago.

11. B. Catton at 60.

succeeded the slain General Johnston.[12] Parvin, however, did not change his low opinion of Grant until the Battle of Vicksburg over a year later, when Grant gained an historic victory.

Most of the soldiers on both sides—including Parvin—had never been in battle before. Some of them ran when faced with the overwhelming danger before them.[13] Parvin mentioned such desertions in one of his letters and threatened to expose the deserters if they did it again.

One prominent Civil War historian has called the Battle of Shiloh "bewildering and bloody," but nonetheless of "decisive importance" because it stopped the Confederacy's "supreme bid to regain western Tennessee" after which "the Confederate path in the West went downhill all the way."[14]

What follows are Parvin's detailed and harrowing accounts of this monumental battle—told from a dog soldier's point of view. These letters are arguably the most dramatic of all the letters in the Parvin collection. The really riveting portions, in the editor's view, have been italicized.

Pittsburg Landing, Tennessee
April 8, 1862

Dear wife,

I set down only for a moment to do as you have requested me to do and that is to write to you if we get into a battle.

We have been into a big fight that lasted two days without intermission. The first day they drove us back about three miles; and then we being reinforced about four o'clock, we commenced to drive them and drove them about half a mile that night. And it got dark, ... so that firing was stopped pretty much for the night. But early next morning it was commenced again and we kept driving them all day. And about two hours before night they broke and run, but I fear that the fight is not over yet.

All seems quiet today. I am not hurt. The rebels had our camp one night and they stole all my things. When I get some paper, I will write you a long letter and I guess I can get some in a day or two.

Yours forever Danl. J. Parvin

---

12. B. Catton at 60.

13. J.M. McPherson at 409. For a comprehensive account of how the raw recruits on both sides handled their first major military engagement, consult: Joseph Allan Frank & George A. Reeves, *Seeing the Elephant: Raw Recruits in the Battle of Shiloh* (University of Illinois paperback) (2003).

14. B. Catton at 60, 63.

Pittsburg Landing, Tennessee
April 14th, 1862

Dear wife and relatives,

I take this opportunity to write to you. I wrote you a short letter after we had the fight to let you know that I was not hurt. And today I shall try and tell you some of the things that happened in our company. I shall not attempt to describe the battle in general for that you can read from the papers in better shape and more correct than I could give them to you.

Our company was formed and marched in line with the rest of the regiments. And we had not been formed but few moments when we were ordered to advance towards the enemy. We had not gone far before we began to hear the balls whistle pretty thick around us. And then we was [p]ut on double quick for about a quarter of a mile. And then we were ordered to halt and form a line of battle. And as soon as we [were] in line, we were ordered to lay down. And about that time the enemy opened fire on us.

When we laid down, Wm Gordon was at my left hand and Wm Mikisell at my right. And we had not fired but once or twice before Gordon was shot through the thigh.[15] *And I looked around and saw that there was some of the boys that would sooner help off with the wounded than fight. So I told Gordon to crawl back and some of the boys would help him off. And then he crawled back and was helped down to the boat.*[16]

And we had not fired but a round or two after that when a ball hit Wm. Mikisell. He said I am shot, carry me back. I put my hand on him and said Bill where are you hit? He made me no answer but turned on his back, and I seen at a glance that it made but little difference to him whether

---

15. William Gordon, age 19, was a resident of Muscatine, Iowa. On October 3, 1861, he enlisted in the army as a private. He was promoted to corporal on November 1, 1861. He was discharged from the army upon expiration of his term of service on October 23, 1864. Roster & Record , 11th Reg. at 327 [this official record does not mention Gordon's injury at Shiloh]; C.W. Soldrs. & Sailrs. ["William Gordon" search].

16. The "boat" was probably located on the Tennessee River behind Union lines.

he was carried back or not.[17] *So I kept on with my shooting, and directly after that, two men was shot almost right behind me. One killed, the other wounded.*

And about that time it was seen that the enemy were flanking us. So we were ordered to fall back, and we fell back about fifty yards and made another stand (some of the boys forgot to stop; I shall not mention any names now). But it was soon found that the enemy were too strong for us. So we were ordered to fall back and we would fall back a piece and make a stand and so the thing kept going.

We had no General at all. General Grant it is said was at Savannah asleep.[18] *One thing is certain he was not with his command. I have no confidence in the man.*

If General Buell[19] had of been in command on Sunday, they would not of drove us back as they did. Buell got here Sunday evening and he sent out word along the lines that if we would keep them in check two hours longer, he would take them off of our hands and let us rest. And from that time we commenced to drive them back. When we had drove them back about half a mile, night came on and fighting was nearly stopped for the night.

And early next morning the firing was commenced (Buell being as good as his word), and he commenced to drive them and we kept driving them all day until almost night and then they broke and run.

---

17. William E. Mikessel, age 20, was a resident of Muscatine, Iowa. On September 21, 1861, he enlisted in the army as a private. On April 6, 1862, he was killed in action at the Battle of Shiloh. Roster & Record, 11th Reg. at 362.

18. Savannah, Tennessee, is located slightly north of Pittsburg Landing on the Tennessee River and was Grant's headquarters during the battle. There was no truth to Parvin's claim, however, that Grant was asleep there and did not take command of the battle. Grant was very active on the field of battle both days; Parvin just never saw him in the huge engagement of Union forces at that time. J.M. McPherson at 407, 409, 412; D.J. Eicher at 226; Richard J. Sommers, "Grant, Ulysses Simpson (1822–1885)," Encyclo. of Civil War 863, 866.

19. General Don Carlos Buell joined Grant on the second day of battle with 25,000 additional troops and helped preserve a Union victory. D.J. Eicher at 229–30. A West Point graduate, General Buell served with distinction in the Mexican War and was in command of the Army of the Ohio at the time of the Shiloh Battle. He participated in a number of battles in the western theater of the Civil War, but, like McClellan, was eventually replaced by Lincoln for pursing the Confederate forces too slowly. Despite the recommendation of Grant, Buell was not later restored to duty; he was perceived to be out of touch with the Union war aims, too sympathetic with the Southern cause, and a political liability. Stephen D. Engle, "Buell, Don Carlos," Encyclo. of Civil War 308–09.

They were in possession of our camp one night and they took everything that I had except my bible and that they abused some. They did not leave me even a change of shirts. They stole all that they could lay hands on, and they robbed the pockets of our dead.

In our company, we had three killed and seventeen wounded. You will see who they are in the paper before you get this. *In walking over the field the day after, the scenes was awful. You could see our men and theirs laying in mangling masses together and dead bodies scattered all over the ground, some with their heads shot entirely off, others with their bodies almost cut in two with cannon balls. But the greater part were killed by small balls. In walking over the field, I saw the dead body of Jim Howal.*[20] *That was the only one out of our company that I knew.*

Now I have wrote all that I have to write about the battle unless I should tell you about some of my narrow escapes. *Besides having a man taken from both sides of me and two from behind me, one of the boys from behind me shot so close to my head that the powder burned my face and ear. And I turned around and gave them a-talking to about that and I think they were more careful. And one of the boys told me after the fight that he had his gun up and was just a-going to shoot, and I stuck my hand in the way and he did not fire until I got out of the way. If he had of been a little more excited, I might of had my brains knocked out by one of our own men.*

And to tell the truth I had almost as much fear of being shot from some of our men as I was from the enemy—although their balls whistled thick and close on every side. But somehow I thought that my time had not come and I feared but little. And if I had of had a good rifle, I would of made some of them think that I was shooting very careless for I found that I could hold just as steady as if I was shooting at squirrels. I did not shoot as often as some of the other boys. I never shot unless I saw something to shoot at. But a good many of the boys did and in consequence a good many run short of ammunition and when we got out of ammunition we were ordered back to get more and when we got back to the commissary we learned that they had sent everything to the river. So we had to go to the river but [as] we were retiring, we passed another regiment or two coming to our relief. We

---

20. James Howall, age 23, was a resident of Muscatine, but was a member of the Sixteenth Regiment Iowa Infantry, and was not a member of Parvin's regiment. He enlisted in the army as a private on October 18, 1861. He was killed in action at the Battle of Shiloh on April 6, 1862. Roster & Record, 11th Reg. at 1124.

passed them and went to the river and when we got there we found that we had been engaged five hours.

And I run another narrow escape once as we were retreating back (I was walking at a slow pace). A cannon ball (a six pounder) passed so close [by] my left ear that it hurt like forty and it made my ear swell up pretty bad. The ball had not passed me more than [illegible] when it struck a man and cut him nearly in two, and then the ball struck a bank and stopped. It is but little use to get behind a tree to get out of the way of them fellas—for they will pass right through just as if there was nothing in the way. In some places the trees are regularly mowed down and the ground torn up every which way.

On Monday the enemy only retreated about four or five miles beyond our lines and there they made another stand. But they destroyed a bridge so that we could not follow them that night. And that night it commenced to rain and it has rained nearly all the time since until yesterday, and it has made the roads impassable for artillery and it is not thought prudent to attack them without that. So we may look for another big battle as soon as the roads are passable. I suppose that we will all be engaged in that, but I have but little fears as to the result for I have confidence in our generals. Halleck[21] is here and I think that he knows what he is about. There is various rumors about the position of the enemy—where they are now. But you will learn that through the papers better than I can tell you, and so I will say nothing about that.

Well, we have had a big fight and we have beaten them back. (I do not say whipped them for I do not consider them whipped yet) and most of the boys are satisfied with fighting and would be glad if they would not be called on to fight any more. But the most of them are willing to fight if called on. And if we have got to fight any more, we would like to do it soon for nearly all of [us] are a-getting homesick, and I think the sooner we do our big fighting the sooner we will get home. ****

21. General Henry Halleck was the top commander of Union forces in the West and took personal command of the army after the Shiloh battle. He advanced at a glacial pace of 20 miles over the next three weeks to Corinth, Mississippi, in ostensible pursuit of the Confederate troops who successfully evacuated the town when Halleck began shelling operations. D.J. Eicher, at 250–51. Third in his class at West Point and a superior administrator, General Halleck proved ineffective as a field commander. Although elevated later to commander-in-chief of all Union forces, Lincoln eventually replaced him with Grant. John C. Fredricksen, "Halleck, Henry Wager (1815–1872)," Encyclo. of Civil War 908–11.

April 15th/62. *** You wanted me to give you a full account of the first fight that I got into. I have given some things in this letter and *I could give you the names of some men that you know that ran on the day of battle long before we were ordered from the field. But I will not put their names down now, but if we get into another fight and they run and I am spared, I will not promise to keep their names from paper.* And I have not promised them now but I think that it is prudent not to give their names now but if I could see you I would tell you some of them.
***

I remain yours until death Danl. J. Parvin

Pittsburg Landing
April 28th 1862

Dear wife and relatives,

*** *You [Sarah] want to know if I killed any rebels. I do not know. I shot twenty five or thirty times but whether I hit anybody or not I cannot say. You want to know if they did not look pretty when they were a-falling. I say no for I do not glory in the death of any man, not even my enemies, but I would rather they would do right and live.* ***

I remain yours forever   Danl. J. Parvin

Section 3. Corinth, Mississippi Campaign and Aftermath [July 1862–January 1863]

After Shiloh, Parvin, along with a heavy concentration of Union troops, advanced on Corinth, Mississippi, 20 miles directly southwest of Pittsburg Landing. Under the cautious command of General Henry Halleck, they proceeded at an exceptionally slow pace. Parvin, however, had no problem with this glacial advance and commented that he "put full confidence" in Halleck and "am perfectly willing to wait on him until he thinks that he is ready." [May 26, 1862: Camp near Corinth, Miss.]

Ostensibly, some 100,000 Union troops were in pursuit of the Confederate retreat from Shiloh. But by the time they reached Corinth after more than three weeks and began shelling operations, the Confederates had successfully evacuated the town; the Confederates then retreated to Tupelo, Mississippi, some 50 miles to the south.[22] As Parvin wrote upon his arrival in Corinth, "there is no enemy around here that will fight." [June 7, 1862: Corinth, Miss.]

a. Jackson-Bolivar, Tennessee Expedition
[Late August–Early September 1862]

Parvin and his regiment were then encamped around Corinth for the next five months. While there in late August1862, Parvin's company was dispatched to protect certain railroad lines against Confederate attack around Jackson, Tennessee, some 35 miles northwest of Corinth. The company proceeded by rail to Jackson and then south by rail about 25 miles to Bolivar, Tennessee, where they were encamped for a short time.

A few weeks later, they left camp at Bolivar and returned to Jackson for a day to guard the rail lines there. Upon completion of that service, they returned to Bolivar, discovered en route a Confederate unit burning bridges, and engaged them in battle around Medon, Tennessee. After a brief skirmish, the Confederates withdrew. In the encounter, however, Parvin was shot through the left ear, as was another soldier in his company. He was also nearly wounded when a rebel shot hit his gun and ruined it.

The following letters contain Parvin's description of this engagement. The italicized portion of the first letter describes Parvin's battle injury. And the italicized portion of the second letter describes his near-injury when his gun was hit.

Camp near Bolivar
Sept. 7th 1862

Dear wife and relatives,

I take this opportunity to write to you for I have not had a chance for the last week, and my chance to write is very small now. And it is very uncertain whether it will go when it is wrote, for the rebels are between you and me.

Well, since I last wrote, I have had some pretty hard soldiering. Last Sunday morning Company H was called on to go on the cars to Jackson for a guard, for there was danger of the trains being attacked. So we got on board and started. And they found out that the load was too heavy for the locomotive. But they pulled it all to the first station and there they left two cars loaded with cotton. And there was cars

---

22. D.J. Eicher at 250–52.

enough loaded there to make another load. From there we had no more trouble on to Jackson.

And we only stayed there a few moments and started back for the other load. And we run down within one station of where our load was. And there we found out that the rebels were between us and the next station. But we knew but very little about their strength. We could see that they had set a good many bridges on fire. So Co. H and a Company from the 45th Ills. got on the cars and run down to where the bridges were on fire. And there the cars stopped and we all got out.

And some went to putting out the fire and the rest of us went to look after the enemy. And we had not gone far before we found them to our hearts content. The first that we saw of them was a lot of their cavalry crossing the railroad about a mile below us. And directly after that we saw a lot of infantry crossing the road. And our boys fired into them but they kept on. And we had not gone but a little farther before they opened a heavy fire from the brush, and then we knew that we were in an ambuscade. And those men that crossed the road were sent around to cut off our retreat. And we were ordered to retreat to the station. It was no use to fight them there for they numbered about twenty to our one.

They killed one man from Co. H and wounded several from the other company at their first fire. And I do not see how any of us escaped. Well we made good time to the station, and we had not been there but a little while before we saw that they were coming on us in great strength. But we had cotton bales for breastwork and we were determined to give them a good fight before we give up. When we got ready we did not have to wait long before we could see them swarming in every direction. And it was not long before they got close enough to fire upon. It was about four o'clock when the firing began and it was kept up until nearly dark. And they found out that they were a-losing too many men and they withdrew with the intention of burning us out that night. But about that time we received reinforcements from Jackson and they drove them back into the woods and saved us. For there was only a hundred and fifty of us, and the least account that they give of themselves is two thousand.

The place that we fought was Medon Station.[23] I shall not attempt to give you a list of the killed and wounded of the other companies.

---

23. Medon, Tennessee, is located approximately halfway between and Jackson and Bolivar, Tennessee.

But our company lost one killed. His name was Wm. C. Budd; he was second sergeant.[24] And the wounded was Wm H. Hazlet.[25] He was shot through the end of the nose and it cut the skin on his cheek. Sarah you know him for he used to go to school with you; he is not hurt much. *And Russle B. Hare (the Colonels brother)*[26] *and myself— we are both hit exactly alike, both through the left ear. My ear is well now.*

* * *

I remain Yours forever   Danl. J. Parvin

————————

Camp near Corinth Miss
Sept. 16th, 1862

Dear wife and relatives

* * *

In my last letter I gave you an account of our fight, but there was one escape that I made that I believe that I forgot to mention. And that was after I was hit in the ear, I raised my gun up to shoot in front of me and stuck my head up over the cotton bale to see if I could see anybody to shoot at, and a ball struck my gun right in front of my forehead. The ball spoiled my gun entirely, and then I had to get up and go and hunt another gun, which I did. I got some wounded man's gun and that lasted me to the end of the fight. * * *

I remain yours forever   Danl. J. Parvin

————————

24. William C. Budd, age 33, was a resident of Muscatine. He enlisted in the army on October 14, 1861, as a fourth corporal. On May 12, 1862, he was promoted to third sergeant. On August 31, 1862, he was killed in action near Meadow [Medon] Station, Tennessee. Roster & Record, 11th Reg. at 298.

25. William H. Hazelett, age 19, was a resident of Muscatine. He enlisted in the army as a private on September 21, 1861, and re-enlisted as a veteran on January 1, 1864. He was wounded slightly on July 21, 1864, near Atlanta, Georgia. He mustered out of the army on July 15, 1865. Roster & Record, 11th Reg. at 335; C.W. Soldrs. & Sailrs. ["William Hazelett" search]. Apparently, Hazelett's slight wound to his nose and cheek at Medon Station was not worthy of note in this military record.

26. Russell B. Hare, age 25, was a resident of Muscatine. He enlisted in the army as a private on October 6, 1861. He mustered out of the army on October 17, 1864, as his term of service had expired. Roster & Record, 11th Reg. at 335; C.W. Soldrs. & Sailrs. ["Russell Hare" search].

b. Ripley, Mississippi Expedition
[Late September 1862]

In late September 1862, Parvin and his company were sent on another ex-pedition out of Corinth—this one to Ripley, Mississippi, some 40 miles to the southwest. In this mission, they encountered a Confederate force in the vicin-ity of the Hatchie River outside of Ripley. And in a two-day battle, they chased the Confederates to Ripley, where the latter scattered in all directions and suf-fered considerable losses. In this battle, Parvin's company was in a reserve line with another company and did not fire their weapons—although enemy rifle balls flew all around them.

Camp near Corinth
Oct. 15th 1862

Since I last wrote [Sept. 25, 1862] I have seen some middling hard soldiering. The next day after I wrote we were ordered to march, and that night we were ordered to go and lay by a battery as we did not know what moment we might be attacked. So we laid out all night and the next morning after we got here, and the fight lasted for two days, and the slaughter on the rebel side was very great. Our side did not suffer so bad and after they were whipped and driven from the field, we were ordered to follow them. And at the Hatchie River[27] a part of our forces got in ahead of them and gave them another whipping and killed a great many of them. And then their confusion was great, but still we followed them and the road was strewn with their stuff.

I picked up one of their guns. A great deal better one than the one that I had, so I took that and left my old musket. So now I have a good rifle, and one that did once belong to the secessionists. And now they had better keep out of the way of it for I think that it will shoot first rate. If the man that stands behind it only does his duty, it will be a bad gun to stand in front of.

Well, we followed them to Ripley, that is about forty miles from Corinth, and then they scattered in every direction so that it was no use in following them any further, so we turned and came back here. And I tell you that we are a dirty lousy set of boys. And we are about three miles from water. But we will try and get to water as fast as we can get leave, and clean up a little. But we do not know but that we

---

27. The Hatchie River flows north/south between Corinth and Ripley, Mississippi.

may be ordered to march in an hour's notice, so it makes it bad about leaving camp. The boys are generally middling well and stood the march first rate. I feel first rate if I only had a chance to wash and get on some clean clothes.

I will not tell you anything about the fight, for you will [read] about that through the papers better than I can tell you. It will be enough for me to tell you that the eleventh was not engaged in the fight at all. That is, not in front but we were held in reserve. And the enemy were within one line of ours several times. And we expected to be called in every moment. But the line in front of us was too strong for them and they had to give back every time. And so that kept us out of the thickest of the fight. But their balls flew over our heads at times pretty thick.

I was tickled at our preacher (Remington).[28] One time when the balls were a-flying over pretty thick, he was setting down by the side of a tree and a ball struck the tree away over his head. And he looked up and then he crawled around to the other side of the tree, preferring the sunny side rather than the side where the bullets were striking. And I did not blame him much for that. But it looked funny to see him crawl around. There was one killed and three wounded in our regiment but none in company H.

* * *

Yours truly and forever,   Danl. J. Parvin

Section 4. Vicksburg Campaign and Aftermath [January 1863–March 1864]

Parvin and his regiment next participated in the historic Vicksburg campaign that resulted in the fall of Vicksburg, Mississippi, on July 4, 1863—coincidentally the same date as the Union victory at Gettysburg. Prior thereto, in November 1862, Parvin and his regiment marched from Corinth, Mississippi into Tennessee, then south into Mississippi, and finally north to Memphis, Tennessee, arriving there in January 1863. Thereafter they were transported by steamboat south on the Mississippi River to a point on the river just north of Vicksburg. For the next six months, Parvin and his company were deployed

---

28. Chauncey [Charing?] H. Remington was appointed Chaplain for the Eleventh Regiment Iowa Infantry on June 25, 1862. He resigned this position on August 7, 1863. Roster & Record, 11th Reg. at 285; Soldrs. & Sailrs. ["Charing Remington" search].

at various places to the south and east of Vicksburg, where skirmishes with the rebels ensued. These events continued until Vicksburg eventually fell.

Although Parvin was involved only as part of the reserve back-up forces, his account of the campaign told from his perspective gives a flavor of how the average soldier experienced this most important Union victory—one that General Ulysses S. Grant later in his memoirs called the turning point of the Civil War.[29] Parvin experienced some rifle and artillery fire during this campaign in nearby battles, but saw no direct action.

One of the many battles that preceded the fall of Vicksburg took place at Big Black River northeast of Vicksburg in May 1863—a scene that Parvin, a month later, was encamped near. Figure 13 is a photograph of the scene of this battle taken in February 1864, some nine months after the battle; Figure 14 is a photograph taken the same month of a Union station established at Big Black River.

After the fall of Vicksburg, Parvin and his regiment remained encamped in the area for some eight months, doing primarily garrison work protecting Vicksburg from potential Confederate guerilla attack. The following letters recount Parvin's part in the great Vicksburg campaign and its lengthy aftermath.

Figure 13. Big Black River Battle Scene Near Vicksburg, Mississippi

Courtesy of the Library of Congress, Civil War Collection.

---

29. "This news [the Vicksburg victory], with the victory at Gettysburg won the same day, lifted a great load of anxiety from the minds of the President, his Cabinet and the loyal people all over the North. The fate of the Confederacy was sealed when Vicksburg fell. Much hard fighting was to be done afterwards and many precious lives were to be sacrificed; but the morale was with the supporters of the Union cause ever after." U.S. Grant, *Personal Memoirs of U.S. Grant* 352 (orig. ed. 1885) (Barnes & Noble paperback ed.) (2003).

Figure 14. Big Black River Union Station Near Vicksburg, Mississippi

Courtesy of the Library of Congress, Civil War Collection.

Camp near Vicksburg
Jan. 26th 1863

Beloved wife and relatives

* * *

Well, we had a very cold disagreeable passage down the [Mississippi] river to this place and now we are camped on the levee about eight or ten miles above Vicksburg on the Louisiana side or opposite the mouth of the Yazoo river.[30] And we can occasionally hear the boom of the big guns at Vicksburg trying to shell our boys whilst they are at work on the canal.[31] And I understand that they throw some shells

30. The Yazoo River flows in a southwesterly direction through the state of Mississippi into the Mississippi River at a point a few miles north of Vicksburg.

31. See Chapter 4, Section 4b, infra, of this work for a discussion of the Union effort to build a canal [Grant's Canal] from the Mississippi River to nearby Lake Providence on the Louisiana side of the river to facilitate the transport of infantry troops to a point south of Vicksburg so as to avoid Vicksburg's big guns on the Mississippi—an effort that ultimately failed. The canal work was carried out some 35 miles north of Vicksburg on the

pretty close, but I guess that they cannot do much hurt at that distance.

* * *

Remaining Yours forever Danl. J. Parvin

June 1st 1863
Haines Bluffs

Dear Wife and Relatives,

I again set down and attempt to write you a few lines to let you know that I am well. When I last wrote, I was at Grand Gulf[32] and the regiment was at Vicksburg. And the next day after I wrote I started to the regiment, and we got there the next day. And I found that the regiment had been in a little skirmish and had one man killed and one wounded, both from Co. D. We got to the regiment just as our Co. and Co. I were going on picket. So we went out with them.

And the rebels kept throwing shell at us all next day, but they did not hurt anybody. They threw most of their shell over us but a good many burst middling close to us. And the next day we laid still and rested. And the next day we started on a long tramp after some rebels that was supposed to be some place back in the country, and now we have traveled some eighty or ninety miles and have not found any that amounts to much.

Our cavalry found a few and skirmished with them a while and they hoisted the white flag and our boys started up to them. And when they got up pretty close, they fired on our boys, killing two and wounding two and then they run. The treacherous villains. They betray first their country and then the flag of truce. And this is not the first time.

And yet these same men have sympathizers at the north and they are worse than a southern rebel, for if it had not of been for them, we should not have any southerners in arms against their country this

---

Mississippi River—and some 25–30 miles north of where Parvin was located when he wrote the above letter.

32. Grand Gulf, Mississippi, is located a short distance south of Vicksburg on the Mississippi River.

day, and there is getting less of them every day. For Pemberton,[33] the commander at Vicksburg, the other [day] asked for a cession of hostilities for six hours to bury his dead, and it was granted him. And then they took advantage of that and come out and captured some of our pickets. The traitorous villains and yet they have sympathizers, but I can assure you that I am not one. I despise them. Their negro slaves are respectable and honorable men when compared with them.

Did I say slaves, well thank God they are slaves no more. They are flocking to our lines by hundreds willing to do anything for their freedom. And they are being armed as soldiers, and they will be used as soldiers to help put down this unjust rebellion.

Vicksburg still holds out against us but our army are throwing shell in there all the time. And they are entirely surrounded so that they will have to come out of their entrenchments to fight us. And we are ready for them at anytime that they may choose, but I think that they will surrender before they will do that.

* * *

I close ever remaining yours
    Danl. J. Parvin

June 7th 1863
Camp near Vicksburg

Dear wife and relatives,

I again attempt to write you a few lines to let you know how we are a-getting along. Well, we have not got Vicksburg yet. I saw in the Muscatine papers that we had possession of the place, but we have not found it out down here yet, but we find it to the contrary. And I do not think that it is a-going to be a very easy matter to take the place yet, but time will tell. Well, we are again close to the enemy, where

---

33. General John C. Pemberton was in command of the Confederate forces at Vicksburg. W. Groom, at 173, 287–92, 294–98. On May 16–17, 1863, Pemberton engaged Grant in two battles outside Vicksburg at Champion's Hill and Big Black Bridge, but was defeated in both encounters. Thereafter, Pemberton retreated to positions in and around Vicksburg for his ultimate unsuccessful defense of the city. "Pemberton, John Clifford," Encyclo. of Civil War 1476, 1478.

we can hear the constant roar of guns, and it seems strange if things gets quiet for a few moments.

* * *

I remain yours forever Danl. J. Parvin

June 22nd 1863
Camp 11th Iowa

Dear wife and relatives

I again set down and attempt to write you a few lines to let you know that I am well. Since I last wrote, we have advanced our lines about two miles. And for the last three days there has been dreadful hard fighting on the wings of our army but the center has only had skirmishing, and we are near the center but still we are exposed to their shells. They have thrown several shells into our camp today but I have not heard of anybody getting hurt by them today.

There is various reports about the success of our army but you will get that in the papers in better shape than I can give it to you, so I will say nothing about it. But one thing is certain. There has been hard fighting and it is still going on, and when that is the case, somebody is in danger of getting hurt. And still they continue to shell our camp. I am afraid that they will hurt somebody yet if they do not stop soon. But that is what we have to expect from them and they have got to look out for themselves for we generally throw two shells to their one.

They have chosen a very strong place to fight us here. They are on high hills and in the woods and we have to advance through open fields and drive them from their fortified positions. And then we take possession of the works that they leave and turn them against them. But we must necessarily lose a good many men in driving them from their strong places. But still the thing goes on. But I think that this summer it will about play out. I hope it will at all events.

* * *

I remain yours as ever   Danl. J. Parvin

July 5th, 1863
In camp near Black River[34]

Dear wife and relatives

I again set down to let you know that I am well. Since I last wrote, things in this part of the country are somewhat changed, for Vicksburg is now in our hands. But you will hear all about that before this gets there and so I will say no more about that.

* * *

But the news caused the Fourth of July[35] to pass off quite pleasantly considering that we were soldiers and on picket and in sight of the enemy. But we feared them not.

I close ever remaining yours,   Danl. J. Parvin

In February 1864, Parvin finally saw some combat action. In the following letter, Parvin briefly describes an expedition he and his brigade participated in that proceeded directly east from Vicksburg, driving Confederate forces to Meridian, Mississippi, near the Mississippi/Alabama border, until the city was captured and virtually destroyed. Parvin states that Union forces took prisoners, recruited 2,000–3,000 African-American soldiers, and destroyed all the public property they could find, including railroad lines. The expedition was under the command of General William T. Sherman.[36] And, as one authority has noted, this campaign "was the first concerted, organized effort at total warfare, wherein the military might of the North was launched against the will of the Southern people as well as military and transportation facilities."[37]

March 5th 1864
Vicksburg Miss

Dear wife and relatives

I again set down and attempt to write you a few lines. * * * I have not time to tell you much about the trip. But I will just say that we com-

---

34. The Big Black River flows to the northeast and east of Vicksburg and empties into the Mississippi River just south of Vicksburg.

35. As stated previously, Vicksburg fell July 4, 1863.

36. Timothy B. Smith, "Meridian Campaign (3 February–4 March 1864)," Encyclo. of Civil War at 1323–24. See D. Eicher at 635–36; Roster & Record, Hist. Skch. at 280.

37. Timothy B. Smith, ibid. at 1323.

menced to drive the rebels soon after we crossed Black River, and we drove them about forty miles beyond Meridian, and we had some middling hard skirmishing with them, and we killed some and took some prisoners. And I should think that we recruited two or three thousand African soldiers. And we destroyed their railroad and destroyed all the public property that we could find.

* * *

So I close ever remaining yours   Danl. J. Parvin

Section 5. Atlanta Campaign and Aftermath [May–September 1864]

In April 1864, after re-enlisting for three more years as a veteran, Parvin was given a 30-day furlough and returned to Muscatine.[38] Thereafter, in May 1864, he was transported from Iowa by steamboat south on the Mississippi River, east on the Ohio River, and south on the Tennessee River, until he reached Clifton, Tennessee, a short distance north of Pittsburg Landing, Tennessee. From that point forward, Parvin marched with his brigade through Tennessee, Alabama, and Georgia—to the outskirts of Atlanta, Georgia. From June to September 1864, Parvin was engaged in a series of skirmishes and fierce battles under the command of General William T. Sherman that eventually led to the fall of Atlanta on September 2, 1864.[39] Two of these furious battles were at Kennesaw Mountain and Nickajack Creek, Georgia, northwest of Atlanta, in late June and early July 1864.[40] See Figure 15 for a photograph taken of General William T. Sherman in a captured Confederate fort taken sometime in 1864 during the Atlanta campaign.

In the last military engagement he participated in on August 20, 1864, outside of Atlanta, Parvin was horribly injured when his jaw and almost all his teeth were shot off. Profusely bleeding, he was taken to a military hospital in the field and was basically left to die. But he didn't die. He was transported to a military hospital in nearby Marietta, Georgia, where he rallied. After a long convalescence, he was discharged from the army on February 25, 1864. See Figure 16 for a typical Union field hospital [Savage Station, Va.], probably similar to the field hospital that Parvin was initially taken to.

---

38. Roster & Record, Hist. Skch. at 280–81.

39. B. Catton at 219–23.

40. Roster & Record, Hist. Skch. 281; Encyclo. of Civil War "Kennesaw Mountain, Battle of (27 June 1864)" 1114–16.

Figure 15. Union General William T. Sherman at a Captured Confederate Fort in the Atlanta Campaign

Courtesy of the Library of Congress, Civil War Collection.

The following letters recount the final bloody encounters that Parvin participated in during the pivotal Atlanta campaign. Amazingly, several of these letters [June 29, July 6, August 12] appear to have been written near the thick of battle, perhaps because Parvin wanted the letters to be found on his body and sent to his wife in case he was killed.

June 16th 1864
Camp 11th Iowa

Dear wife and relatives

I again set down and attempt to write you a few lines. Since I last wrote, we have advanced about fifteen miles and yesterday we had some of the hardest skirmishing that I ever saw. It almost amounted

Figure 16.　Union Field Hospital in Virginia, June 1862

Courtesy of the Library of Congress, Civil War Collection.

to a battle. The eleventh suffered considerable. Wm Tailor[41] of our company was severely wounded. I think in all probability that he is dead by this time (but that I do not know). Some of the companies that were thrown forward as skirmishers lost severely. We gained one line of their works and we hold them this morning. The rebels tried to retake them last night but they failed and our men fortified themselves last night. So I think they will hold their position, although there is severe skirmishing going on at this time, and we are liable to be called out at any moment. But as we were under fire all day yesterday, I think that they will allow us to rest today unless they should press our front line too hard. And if that should be the case, we are all ready and willing to go at any moment.

41. William G. Taylor, age 39, was a resident of Muscatine. He enlisted in the army as a private on March 12, 1864. He was wounded severely, but did not die, on June 15, 1864, near Kennesaw Mountain, Georgia. He mustered out of the army on July 15, 1865. Roster & Record, 11th Reg. at 393; C.W. Soldrs. & Sailrs. ["William Taylor" search].

The rebels have two lines of works yet in front of us that we know of and perhaps some that we do not know of yet, but I guess that we will find them before long. They have the advantage of us here for they have had the choice of their ground and they have chosen a strong position, but still our men keeps steadily advancing on them. Our forces captured a good many prisoners yesterday. They seem very much discouraged about their cause, and seem very well satisfied as prisoners. I have just heard that Tailor is not dead yet! * * *

I remain Yours forever Danl. J. Parvin

June 29th 1864
Camp 11th Iowa

Dear wife and relatives

I again set down and attempt to write you a few lines. We are nearly in the same place where we were when I last wrote, and the rebels continue to shell us occasionally, but they have done but little damage in that way. But still it makes it disagreeable for us to lay under the range of their guns and have their shells bursting around us.

Since I last wrote, we have been in another pretty tight place. (I shall only speak as far as our company is concerned.) We were on picket on the night of the 26th and on the morning of the 27th. We were ordered to charge their works, and about 11 o'clock the line of skirmishers commenced to advance. And as soon as [we] got in sight of them, they let a volley into us but most of the balls passed over our heads and done but little hurt in our company (but the 16th suffered severely). But it gave us to understand that they numbered two to our one, and they were entrenched and we were in the open field. And we seen that if we advanced we would all be killed, so we fell back to the edge of the timber and there we laid until night. When we were relieved, nearly all of the line fell back to our works where they started from.

Two of our company were wounded. Their names are Ufford[42] and Wilhelm,[43] both of them recruits and I tell you that the recruits stood up to the work bravely. Parvin[44] says that he did not like it very well, but he could not think of running until the rest did. * * *

I remain Yours   Danl. J. Parvin

———————

July 6th 1864
Camp 11th Iowa

Dear wife and relatives

I again set down whilst the noise of musketry and the boom of cannon is constantly sounding in my ear and attempt to write you a few lines. Since I last wrote, we have seen a good deal of war and its effects. We have moved about 15 miles to the left of where we were when I last wrote. We marched all of one night and nearly all of the next day in order to get in our position. And then our brigade had to drive the rebels off, and we have drove them about 5 miles since we took up our position on the right. We have done most of our marching in line of battle through the brush and in some places the brush was dreadful thick so that it was almost impossible to get through.

I will now try to tell you how some of us spent our Fourth (I shall only tell you about Co. H.). Well, we were detailed on the Fourth for picket duty, so we went out and about noon we were ordered to join

———————

42. Thomas Ufford, age 18, was a resident of Port Louisa, Iowa [does not appear on modern Iowa maps, but at the time probably a small village in Louisa County, located to the south of Muscatine County]. Ufford enlisted in the army as a private on March 29, 1864. Shortly thereafter, on June 27, 1864, he was severely wounded near Kennesaw Mountain, Georgia. He recovered and was mustered out of the army on July 15, 1865. Roster & Record, 11th Reg. at 394; C.W. Soldrs. & Sailrs. ["Thomas Ufford" search].

43. Simon P. Wilhelm, age 26, was a resident of Muscatine. He was mustered into the army as a private on December 9, 1863. He was severely wounded on June 27, 1864, near Kennesaw Mountain, Georgia. He recovered and was discharged from the army on July 20, 1865. Roster & Record, 11th Reg. at 402; C.W. Soldrs. & Sailrs. ["Simon Wilhelm" search].

44. Daniel Parvin is referring to his young nephew, William Parvin Freeman, the son of J.P. Freeman and Parvin's sister Lydia. U.S. Census, Muscatine County, Iowa, Household of J.P. Freeman (Sept. 4, 1850). William Parvin Freeman, age 19, enlisted in the army as a private on January 28, 1864, and was later promoted to second corporal. He mustered out of the army on July 15, 1865. Roster & Record, 11th Reg. at 323; C.W. Soldrs. & Sailrs. ["William Freeman" search].

our regiment and advance. We done so, and we had gone but a short distance when we were ordered to relieve our skirmishers and drive the enemy. We relieved our skirmishers, and we charged on the enemy's works (made of rails) and drove them back and followed them up. And in about a half mile we found out that they had another line of works made of rails and we charged on them with a yell and they left in a hurry. And we followed them up and drove them from their third line of works, and still we followed them up to their fourth line of works. And we found that they had strong earthworks and more men than we had, but we charged up to within about one hundred yards of their works, and they opened two pieces of artillery on us charged with grapeshot and canister that was middling severe on us. Hawley of our Co. was killed by a grapeshot.[45] I was about one hundred yards from the rebels works, and I had some first rate shots at them, and I expect that somebody got hurt. Parvin[46] was very cool all the time, and in fact all the boys done first rate.

After dark we were ordered to withdraw, and we fell back a piece that night. And the next morning we charged their works and took them and followed them up to this place. And here they have the strongest works that I have seen in the south, and they seem determined to hold them.

July 7. This is early in the morning and things goes on about as usual. The weather is very warm. The boys are in good spirits generally and expect to take Atlanta before we get rest. As the mail goes out this morning, I shall have to bring my letter to a close.

Yours as ever   Danl. J. Parvin

———————

The italicized portion of the following letter describes a hair-raising battle involving Parvin and his brigade in which he narrowly escaped injury when a rebel ball whizzed by his neck and split his collar.

———————

45. William A. Hawley, age 18, was a resident of Muscatine. He enlisted in the army as a private on February 26, 1864. Shortly thereafter, on July 1, 1864, he was killed in action at Nickajack Creek, Georgia. He was buried in a National Cemetery in Marietta, Georgia, Section F, Grave 544. Roster & Record, 11th Reg. at 335; C.W. Soldrs. & Sailrs. ["William Hawley" search].

46. William Parvin Freeman, age 19, was Parvin's nephew.

July 24th 1864
Camp 11th Iowa near Atlanta

Dear wife and relatives

I again set down and attempt to let you know how I am a getting along. I am well this morning and my legs have got about well, so that I am in hopes that I shall be able to stand it now.

Since I last wrote we have been in another terrible battle, but I shall not attempt to describe it to you. Only a few things that I saw, and I will commence on the morning of the 21st. We had been building breastworks that night and we were ordered forward and we advanced to the next line of works. This line was occupied by the 13th and 16th [Regiments]. They advanced towards the enemy's works. They advanced part of the way and were compelled to fall back. Soon after that, the left wing of our regiment were ordered forward as skirmishers. Our company were in this. We went up to within about two hundred yards of their works and commenced to entrench ourselves. And I tell you that the bullets came thick. Well, we got our trench just about done when we were ordered to leave and go further to the left. So we moved about a half mile to the left and threw up breastworks there.

And early on the morning of the 22nd, we heard musketry firing in our rear and we knew at once that they had flanked us, but we were determined to meet them in any shape. They came closer and closer until we found that they were on three sides of us and within about a hundred yards of us and closing in on our open side, so we were compelled to fall back. And we fell back a short distance and fought them first on one side of our works and then on the other. And so we fought them all day.

And in the evening as we were retiring from the front, we passed over a part of the battlefield, and in some places the dead rebels laid so thick that it was difficult to walk without treading on them. So that I think that their movement cost them pretty dearly, but you will hear all about that in the papers.

They came close enough to me to cut my shirt collar in two, and the ball rubbed my neck a little but it did not break the skin. Yesterday was spent in burying the dead. And today we are a-getting ready for action, and I must stop writing and help.

Well, we have got ready and now I will try and finish my letter. Our company lost in the fight on the 22nd, seven in wounded and missing. The missing we do not know whether they are killed or taken prisoners. There are three wounded and four missing. The names of the wounded are Ady,[47] Hyink,[48] [and] Nuson;[49] the missing: Jackson,[50] Brochart,[51] Sparks,[52] and Coe[53] and we fear that they are killed.

The rebels hold that part of the battlefield, but we hold the greater part of the field that we fought over. And we had a great many of their dead to bury, and I am in hopes that they will bury our dead as respectably as we did theirs. * * *

I remain yours as ever Danl. J. Parvin

The italicized portions of the following letter is a chilling foreshadowing of the terrible, near-fatal injury to his face and jaw that Parvin would suffer eight days later. The letter was clearly written in the thick of battle probably be-

47. William D. Ady, age 20, was a resident of Atalisa, Iowa. He enlisted in the army as a private on October 14, 1861, and re-enlisted as a veteran on January 1, 1864. He was wounded slightly in the right arm near Atlanta, Georgia, on July 22, 1864. He mustered out of the army as a sergeant on July 15, 1865. Roster & Record, 11th Reg. at 290; C.W. Soldrs. & Sailrs. ["William Ady" search].

48. Henry Hyink, age 21, was a resident of Muscatine, although originally from Holland. He enlisted in the army as a private on February 15, 1864. Several months later, on July 4, 1864, he was wounded at Nickajack Creek, Georgia. A few weeks later, on July 22, 1864, he was taken prisoner near Atlanta, Georgia. He survived his imprisonment and mustered out of the army on June 2, 1865. Roster & Record, 11th Reg. at 335; C.W. Soldrs. & Sailrs. ["Henry Hyink" search].

49. John Nason, age 22, was a resident of Muscatine, although originally from Holland. He enlisted in the army as a private on February 24, 1864. He was wounded in the right leg near Atlanta, Georgia, on July 22, 1864. He mustered out of the army on July 15, 1865. Roster & Record, 11th Reg. at 366; C.W. Soldrs. & Sailrs. ["John Nason" search].

50. Silas Jackson, age 30, was a resident of Muscatine. He enlisted in the army as a private August 15, 1862. He was killed in action on July 22, 1864, near Atlanta, Georgia. Roster & Record, 11th Reg. at 340; C.W. Soldrs. & Sailrs. ["Silas Jackson" search].

51. Although there was no one named Brochart in the Eleventh Iowa Infantry, Parvin may have been referring to Samuel Bozarth, age 26, who was a resident of Tipton, Iowa. He enlisted in the army as a private on August 30, 1862, and was mustered out on June 2, 1865. Roster & Record , 11th Reg. at 298; C.W. Soldrs. & Sailrs. ["Samuel Bozarth" search].

52. William P. Sparks, age 20, was a resident of Muscatine. He enlisted in the army as a private on October 3, 1861, and was promoted to fourth corporal on June 6, 1863. He was missing in action near Atlanta on July 22, 1864. He survived and was mustered out of the army on July 15, 1865. Roster & Record, 11th Reg. at 387; C.W. Soldrs. & Sailrs. ["William Sparks" search].

53. Justine E. Coe, age 21, was a resident of Muscatine. He enlisted in the army as a private on September 21, 1861. He was promoted to seventh corporal on October 1, 1862. He was taken prisoner near Atlanta, Georgia, on July 22, 1864. He survived and mustered out of the army on June 2, 1865. Roster & Record, 11th Reg. at 306.

cause—as previously noted—Parvin wanted the letter to be found on his body and sent to his wife in case he was killed.

Aug. 12th 1864
Camp 11th Iowa near Atlanta

Dear Wife and Relatives

As this is my birthday, I thought that I would spend a part of it in writing to you. It has not been quite a week since I wrote to you, but most likely our company will be on picket tomorrow, so that I should not have a chance to write for two days. For the pickets have all that they can attend to, to watch the enemy, for our lines are getting pretty close together, and they keep up nearly a constant firing on both sides, and there is a good many killed and wounded every day by this way.

And now whilst I am writing, the balls are almost constantly whistling past me, and occasionally one will strike a soldier that happens to be in its course. But such are the effects of war, and we get used to such things and pay but little attention to them.

The rebels shell us nearly all the time here and I tell you that the sound of their shell as they pass through the air—and frequently they burst close to us scattering their fragments among us—I say that the sound of these missiles as they pass through the air is not very pleasant to the ear, for we cannot tell where they are a-going to strike. And perchance they strike the man next to you, and we do not know but what our turn may be next, but that is a chance that we all run for the sake of our country. * * *

Sarah, you speak about somebody turning that ball from my neck. I could not see that it was turned at all and my shirt collar did not turn it as I could see. I wish that the next one would be turned off before it comes quite so close.

The rebels attacked our pickets three times last night and we were called up in line of battle each time. But at such a time it does not take us long to get into line and ready for a fight. But I would rather fight them in the daytime if it should suit them, for I can see how to shoot better by daylight.

But we will try and be ready for them at all times, for we cannot tell at what time the traitorous villains will be upon us. But as loyal men defending our country's rights, we will meet them and endeavor to do our duty to our country and trust to Providence for the result. And I trust that all will be right in the end.

I remain yours until death   Danl. J. Parvin

Sept. 6th 1864
Marietta [Georgia] Hospital

Dear wife

I again undertake to let you know that I am yet counted among the living, and not only that but I am considered doing well. And I think that if nothing else sets in, I shall be able to stand it through this trip. *But Sarah I shall be a dreadful homely man when I get well for they took out so much of my jawbone that it will let my cheeks and lips settle in and my teeth are about all gone, and there is various other ailments too numerous to mention now.* It will be some time before I shall be able to travel, and I do not know whether they intend to send me north or not. But I hope that they will. Time will tell these things.

Well, I am getting tired setting up and shall have to stop writing. Ever remaining yours

Danl. J. Parvin

In the following letter, Parvin describes how he received his near-fatal wound and was taken to a nearby military field hospital, profusely bleeding, where he was briefly examined and basically left to die. Although not free from doubt, it is likely that Parvin was hit in a minor skirmish as his regiment proceeded in a sweep around the west of Atlanta to the city's southern outskirts [from which Sherman's forces ultimately entered the city on September 2, 1864].[54] The portions of the letter that the editor considers the most dramatic have been italicized.

---

54. Shelby Foote. *The Civil War, A Narrative: Red River to Appomattox* 520–29 (Vintage Books, Div. of Random House) (paperback) (1986); J.M. McPherson at 754–55, 774; D.J. Eicher at 712–13.

As an aside, however, the only *official* battle fought by the Union Army around Atlanta on August 20, 1864 [the date Parvin was hit], was at Lovejoy Station and Jonesboro, Georgia, on the southern outskirts of Atlanta. This battle was waged by Union cavalry units—not by Union infantry units—and consequently Parvin's infantry unit could not have been involved. Shelby Foote, ibid. at 520–21; Frederick Phisterer, *Statistical Record of the Armies of the United States* 188–89 (Charles Scribners Sons) (1888).

Sept. 12th 1864
Hospital 17th A.C. Marietta [Georgia]

Dear wife and relatives

    I again undertake to write you a few lines so that you may know how I am a-getting along. I am improving just as fast as a man can with such a wound as I have got (so says the Doctors). I will try to give you a history of myself as I remember things from the time that I was shot until now.

    When the ball struck me, I was squatting down close to the breastworks. When the ball first struck me, I thought that my head was gone, and then the boys commenced to collect around me. And then I got over on my knees and put my hand up to my face. And I could hear the boys talking and I could think. And I know by that, that I was not shot through the brain and they asked me if I could walk. I told them yes. And they took hold of me and led me back about two hundred yards, and there we met the boys coming with the stretcher. And I got into that and they carried me to the division hospital. And there was three or four doctors there, but most of them shook their heads when they saw me and did not seem inclined to do anything for me.[55]

    But finally, as they had nothing else to do, they thought that they would see if there could be anything done for me. So they got me on their chopping block and gave me chloroform, but it had but little effect on me for I knew all that was going on all the time. And they took out several loose pieces of bone and one good big piece of my jawbone, it having four teeth on it. After that, they let me go back to my bunk. I believe that they thought that I would bleed to death, and I guess that I did come pretty near it. Well, I laid there and bled all night.

---

    55. The circumstances leading to this dreadful injury are more particularly described in the tribute to Daniel J. Parvin upon the latter's death. Register of Old Settlers 92. According to this source, Captain George O. Morgridge [a fellow soldier and Parvin's physician during Parvin's last illness] had fired a shot at two rebel soldiers whose forms could be seen occasionally above the Confederate's nearest fortification. One of these rebel soldiers returned fire. The shot struck a pole on which Captain Morgridge was resting his gun and then freakishly glanced downward—striking Parvin who was ostensibly out of the range of fire and seated nearby.

    Captain Morgridge, age 21, was a resident of Muscatine. He enlisted in the army as a private on October 18, 1861. He was promoted to first corporal on November 1, 1862. He re-enlisted as a veteran on January 1, 1864. He was then promoted to first sergeant and was serving in this capacity at the time of Parvin's injury. He was promoted to captain on November 15, 1864, and later was discharged on July 15, 1865. Roster & Record, 11th Reg. at 33.

And the next day they sent me here. And they fed me with a stomach tooth [tube?] for two or three days, but I found out that I was a-going to starve if I did not find out some other way besides that. So I concluded that I would try some other plan. And I found that by holding my nose that I could drink a little and that is the way that I have to do yet. And I cannot eat anything, only what I can drink, but I can drink almost anything now. But the most of my living is gruel, but I can drink that quite thick now. My appetite is good.

They have taken my name for a furlough, but how soon it will come I cannot tell, but I hope as soon as I am able to travel. As I have filled my sheet full, I close ever remaining yours

    Danl. J. Parvin

Marietta [Georgia] Hospital
Sept. 26, 1864

Dear wife and relatives * * *

Rob. Ingersoll[56] was here to see me. He has been like a brother to me. He brought me up the ball that passed through my head, and the piece of jawbone that was taken from me. He said that he had just been to the regiment and that the boys were looking well and in good spirits. He expects to get his discharge about the middle of the month. * * *

Yours   Danl. J. Parvin

Marietta [Georgia] Hospital
Oct. 3rd 1864

Dear wife and relatives * * *

My wound is nearly healed up and I feel very well nearly all the time. But *I cannot use my jaw but very little and I guess I will never be able to*

---

56. Robert Ingersoll, age 25, was Parvin's best friend in the army. Ingersoll was a resident of Muscatine. He enlisted in the army as a fifth sergeant on October 12, 1861. He was promoted to second sergeant on October 1, 1862, and later to first sergeant on November 1, 1862. He mustered out of the army on October 14, 1864, upon completion of his term of service. Roster & Record, 11th Reg. at 337.

use it much again. And if that be the case, how will I manage to eat green corn? I have often thought of that since I have been hurt. And I tell you that I shall try and study up some way, for I do love it so well. * * *

Ever remaining Yours   Danl. J. Parvin

Section 6. Other Minor Skirmishes and Expeditions

Parvin had knowledge of other minor skirmishes and expeditions that did not involve him, but which took place near where he was located. As he was close to many military operations and had access to information from fellow soldiers, he was able to write home about these operations. The following are selections from his letters dealing with these matters.

> Our scouting parties have been doing a little. We have taken some seventy-five or a hundred prisoners and nearly provisions enough to keep us. We have sent about twenty-five prisoners to St. Louis. The rest have taken the oath.[57] And our scouts are out nearly every day. Some days they catch one or two of Price's men,[58] and other days they get nothing. [Jan. 28, 1862: California, Mo.]

> Our advance [to Corinth] have had several skirmishes and one considerable of a fight last week with the enemy. But our troops have drove them this far, but they seem to have retreated about as far as they intend to. [April 28, 1862: Pittsburg Landing, Tenn.]

----

57. Union and Confederate soldiers taken prisoner were sometimes paroled to return home upon their promise not to re-join the army—as opposed to being transferred to a prison camp. J.M. McPherson at 791–92. General Grant, in fact, gave such paroles to 30,000 captured Confederate soldiers after the fall of Vicksburg in July 1863. B. Catton at 141. But, for a variety of reasons, that policy changed by the end of 1863; captured soldiers were sent to prison camps and were no longer exchanged or paroled. J.M. McPherson at 792. Nonetheless, at the end of the war in April 1865, General Grant paroled all of the Confederate soldiers who were captured at Appomattox. B. Catton at 260.

58. No doubt Parvin was referring to the Confederate soldiers under General Sterling Price, the commander of the pro-Southern militia in Missouri. Although a slave state, Missouri never seceded and remained in Union hands throughout the Civil War—after some early decisive Union victories. Nonetheless, pro-southern guerillas remained active in Missouri throughout the War. J.M. McPherson at 292–93.

Our soldiers are a-having skirmishes with them every day (almost) and we (that is, our regiment) have orders to be ready to march in a moment's notice. So I do not know what moment we may be led into a fight, and I do not think that the time will be put off much longer. [Nov. 11, 1862: Grand Junction, Tenn.]

When I last wrote, we were at Clinton [Miss.]that is out near Jackson [Miss.]. But as the rebels run from there, it was no use for us to stay out there any longer, and so Genl. Grant's army is being scattered all over the country again. And our brigade is left at the railroad bridge on Big Black [River] for the present. How long we will stay here is very uncertain. We might leave here in an hour, and we might stay near here all summer.

This has been a very nice and expensive bridge over the stream at this place, but when the rebels were driven from here, they burned it and destroyed the road as much as they could, and I do not think that our men will fix it up again. [July 25, 1863: Big Black River, Vicksburg, Miss.]

Sarah, I have but little news to write—only that we are on duty every day and we are expecting to have a fight here soon. And in fact our troops and the rebels are fighting every day now only about twenty miles from here. And it is hard to tell how soon they may come in here or else we go out there to meet them. I suppose that there is some hard fighting to do yet. [Oct. 9, 1863: Vicksburg, Miss.]

Since I last wrote, we have moved out here, but I do not think that we will stay here very long. Our men and the enemy were fighting yesterday twelve miles from here on the road to Jackson [Mississippi]. I do not know how they made it. We may be called out to reinforce them at any moment. [Oct. 17, 1863: Camp near RR Bridge on the Big Black River, Miss.]

Since I last wrote, we have moved into Vicksburg again. I thought when we were out on the Big Black [River] that we should get into a fight. And our troops did have a little skirmishing with the rebels, but they kept running so that our forces could not catch them. [Oct. 25, 1863: Vicksburg, Miss.]

––––––––––

There are a few scattering bands of rebels strolling around over the country and they occasionally capture a steamboat or a few horses or mules. But before we can get there, they are gone. I think that our government will have to adopt a new plan with these southern high-wayman (for they are nothing better than highwayman). I think that we had ought to string them up by the neck as fast as we catch them. [Jan. 15, 1864: Vicksburg, Miss.]

Chapter 3

Opinions of Contemporary People and Events

Parvin peppers his letters with lively and often critical opinions of the events and people of his day—including some very negative views concerning his own commanding officers. Clearly, his letters were never censored. Indeed, in one letter, Parvin flatly states that the officers never dictated to the soldiers what they could write in their letters—except that treasonous expressions against the government were never allowed:

> William,[1] in your letter you want to know if our officers dictate to us soldiers what we shall write. I say most emphatically, no. And I am glad you told some of them that they were d—d liars[2] when they accused our officers of such things. And I will tell you what they do not allow us to talk or write, and that is treason against our government. But thanks to the good sense of the soldiers, there are but few that want to do that. [May 14, 1863: Grand Gulf, Miss.]

What follows are excerpts from Parvin's letters in which he freely expresses his views on a wide range of subjects and people.

Section 1. The Rationale and Politics of the War

Parvin states his emphatic opinions on the following: the justice of the Union cause; the unjustified nature of the Confederate cause; the bravery, ability and disloyalty of the Confederate soldiers; and the absolute treason of Southern sympathizers in the North. As to the latter [frequently called "Copperheads"],

---

1. It is likely that Parvin is replying to a letter from his brother William S. Parvin. William is one of Parvin's more frequent correspondents. Register of Old Settlers at 130.
2. To the editor's knowledge, this is the only time that Parvin used any profanity in his letters—and this usage was mild indeed.

Parvin reserves his most damning invective, as he strongly believed that these people undermined the Northern war effort and were traitors to the country.

Beyond that, Parvin's opinions on these subjects and people became more strident the longer the war dragged on. Time and again, he bitterly lashed out against what he saw as the cause of this rebellion and the people who abetted it. The more he saw the carnage of the war and the slaughter of his comrades-in-arms, the less restrained he was in his outrage.

a. Parvin's Views on the Union Cause

These letters show Parvin's strong sense of duty and patriotism to his country, and his willingness to die for what he saw as a just cause.

> I believe that I am doing right in trying to put down this dreadful rebellion. If it was not for this belief, I can assure you that I should not be soldiering now, for it is anything but a pleasant business to me. And I shall be dreadful glad when this dreadful war is at an end. And when that will be, only He that knows all things can tell. But I sincerely hope that the time is close at hand when our beloved country will be again united and peace and plenty will again take the place of war and its natural consequences, which are misery in all its various forms. * * * I do not think that I could be happy if I was to desert my country whilst she needs my services. I thought so when I re-enlisted, and Sarah, I hope that you will not blame me too hard for doing what I considered my duty. [Jan. 31, 1864: Vicksburg, Miss.]

> Sarah ... I believe that I have one of the best women living, not only saving but kind and prudent. And I am sorry that I came off here and left her. But I thought that I was a-doing my duty. And as far as right and wrong is concerned, I done right, believing as I did that my country needed me. And I feel now as I did then that I would be willing to spend my life's blood for my country if it is necessary. [Feb. 3, 1862: California, Mo.]

> William,[3] you think that I am ready to fight in a better cause than Washington fought in. Yes, I am ready and I think the cause is better.

---

3. Probably Daniel's brother William S. Parvin. Register of Old Settlers at 130.

Yes, I know it is better to fight a traitor than it would be to fight a foreign foe. And all are traitors that sympathize with traitors. [Feb. 26, 1862: California, Mo.]

———————

I feel that I have done my duty to my country. And if I had not of done as I have done, I should feel that I had not done my duty. But I cannot think that I shall be called to sacrifice my life for that country. But if that is necessary, I am ready. [May 26, 1862: Camp near Corinth, Miss.]

———————

I have suffered a good deal for my country, and if necessary I am willing and ready to die for my country if necessary. But I am in hopes that sacrifice will not be required. But there are many that are better than I am that will yet suffer death before this terrible rebellion is put down. [Sept. 21, 1864: Marietta, Ga. Hospital]

b. Parvin's Views on the Confederate Cause

In these letters, Parvin condemns the leaders of the rebellion and wishes that they burn in hell.

I am willing to run my chances in battle if it will bring this unholy rebellion to a close. Oh! The amount of sin that the leaders in this rebellion will have to answer for and for the destruction of human life and happiness beyond my powers of calculation. [April 23, 1862: Pittsburg Landing, Tenn.]

———————

Oh this war, how much misery it has caused this country. And all brought about by a few southern bigots. Oh, how I wish they were in hell (where they belong) and all northern sympathizers with them. [Oct. 15–16, 1862: Camp near Corinth, Miss.]

———————

Wm,[4] in yours you seem to think that the war is drawing to a close. I hope that you are right in that, but I tell you that if it was not for those

———————

4. Probably Daniel's brother William S. Parvin. Register of Old Settlers at 130.

infernal politicians of the Courier stripe,[5] this war would have been at an end long ago. Oh! the black hearted traitors. How I hate them. If it had not of been for them, we would not of had this trouble on us. And since they have got it on, they do all in their power to keep it a-going. Oh! the black hearted villains. If I had the destroying power, I would destroy them all at a stroke and rid the country of treason for once. [Feb. 17, 1863: Lake Providence, La.]

I would sooner serve my life out here than give one inch to the traitors of my country, the impudent scoundrels. I wish that they were all where they belong and that is in hell. [June 16, 1863: Camp near Vicksburg, Miss.]

c. Parvin's Views on Confederate Soldiers

Parvin held ambivalent views on Confederate soldiers. He often admired them for their bravery and fighting ability, and even felt some sympathy for them at times. But he also condemned them as traitors to the country and for specific instances of perfidy on the battlefield. Also Parvin much preferred death to being taken prisoner by the Confederate forces. Still, despite his hatred of the Confederate cause, he did not glory in the death of any rebel soldier. He remained throughout the war a passionate, but decent man.

They [the Confederates] have quite a large army yet, and they are brave men. And Beauregard[6] is a very good general. It is very easy to see the effect of a good general on a battlefield and Beauregard proved himself such here on Sunday. The men under him fought with desperation, but the prisoners that we took said that their officers stood behind them with drawn revolvers and swords and threatened to shoot or cut down the first man that attempted to run. Whether the prisoners

---

5. Parvin was most likely referring to the Muscatine Daily Courier, a Democratic newspaper in Muscatine, and to its publisher Edward Thayer whom Parvin despised as a traitor. Thayer was quite active in the Democratic Party, both then and later. Thayer ran for Congress as a Democrat in 1862, but was defeated. See the letters collected at Section 1d, infra, of this chapter.

6. General P.G.T. Beauregard was one of the Confederate generals in the Battle of Shiloh. When Confederate General Albert Johnston, the commanding general, was killed in the first day of battle, General Beauregard replaced him. J.M. McPherson at 410–11; B. Catton at 60. General Beauregard was also the top Confederate Commander at the firing on Ft. Sumter April 12–14, 1861. Encyclo. of Civil War, "Beauregard Pierre Gustave Toutant (181–1893)"198.

tell the truth or not I cannot tell, but I do know that they fought like brave men. And I could see by their movements that they were well-drilled a great deal better than we were, for they went through with some maneuvers on the battlefield right under our fire that we cannot do right on the drill ground, much less on the battlefield. [April 14, 1862: Pittsburg Landing, Tenn.]

You [Sarah] want to know if I killed any rebels. I do not know. I shot twenty five or thirty times but whether I hit anybody or not I cannot say. You want to know if they did not look pretty when they were a-falling. I say no for I do not glory in the death of any man, not even my enemies, but I would rather they would do right and live. [April 28, 1862: Pittsburg Landing, Tenn.]

But they [the rebel army] are very strong yet and they fight with a courage worthy [of] a better cause. I do not blame the rebel soldier so very much for they say that they are a-fighting for their bread and meat. The rich will go to the poor and tell them that they have got to fight or starve and they fight rather than starve. So said some of the prisoners that we took on the day of the battle. Others are drove into it by threatening to kill them if they do not enlist in the Southern cause. And the prisoner told us that the officers on the battlefield stood behind the men with drawn sword and pistol and swore that they would shoot the first man that offered to run. So under the circumstances it is not much wonder that the men fought brave. They thought that it was better to be shot by us than to be shot by their own officers.

There was one poor wounded rebel that had received his death wound. And as the American flag was carried past him, he looked up at it and said that he thanked God that he was a-going to die beneath the American flag. And I have an idea that there are plenty of rebels that would gladly leave their flag and fight under the stars and stripes if they only knew that they dare. But they were told that we kill all that we get our hands on and their ignorance make them believe anything that their leaders tell them for they cannot read for themselves. And if they could read, they do not have the opportunity, for slavery requires ignorance. [April 28, 1862: Pittsburg Landing, Tenn.]

The next day we started on a long tramp after some rebels that was supposed to be some place back in the country and now we have traveled some eighty or ninety miles and have not found any that amounts to much. Our cavalry found a few and skirmished with them a while and they hoisted the white flag and our boys started up to them and when they got up pretty close, they fired on our boys killing two and wounding two and then they run. The treacherous villains. They betray first their country and then the flag of truce and this is not the first time. * * *

Pemberton, the commander at Vicksburg,[7] the other [day] asked for a cession of hostilities for six hours to bury his dead, and it was granted him. And then they took advantage of that and come out and captured some of our pickets. The traitorous villains and yet they have sympathizers, but I can assure you that I am not one. I despise them. Their negro slaves are respectable and honorable men when compared with them. Did I say slaves, well thank God they are slaves no more. They are flocking to our lines by hundreds willing to do any thing for their freedom. And they are being armed as soldiers, and they will be used as soldiers to help put down this unjust rebellion. [June 1, 1863: Haines Bluff, near Vicksburg, Miss.]

Our men had a skirmish with some of the enemy near this place yesterday morning, and we took nine prisoners and two of the nine were paroled at Vicksburg since the Fourth of July. So you see there is no honor in them. But we do not give them a chance to fight us another time for we make them go dead in short order. They and their supposed government are no better than pirates, and had ought to be treated as pirates. [July 17, 1863: Clinton, Miss., near Vicksburg, Miss.]

I would almost as leave die as to be taken prisoner by them [Confederates]. Thank fortune that has never fallen for my lot, and I hope it never will. To be taken prisoner by a lot of fiends that would dare to raise their hands against the best government that ever existed without the slightest cause, I can hardly bear the idea. And I think that between prisoner with them and death, there is but little choice. And

---

7. General John C. Pemberton was the Confederate commanding general during the Vicksburg campaign. W. Groom at 173, 287–92, 294–98.

they are all for McClellan[8] and that makes me hate him and all those that would try to ruin their country by voting for him, but I suppose there are some such. Now I will tell you what I think of such men. *They are either very ignorant or else they are traitors for this is a time that admits of no middle ground.*[9] [Oct. 15, 1864: Marietta, Ga. Hospital]

Immediately after the Battle of Vicksburg, Daniel Parvin ran across a Confederate prisoner named Parvin from Texas. This soldier claimed that Daniel's father was his uncle [which would make him Daniel's cousin].[10] The soldier sent word that he wanted to see Daniel. But Daniel refused as he did not want to claim a relationship "with any man in arms against the laws of his country." Later, however, Parvin regretted that decision.

Sarah, when we (I mean our division) were coming from Jackson [Mississippi] the last time, we had in our charge between five and six hundred prisoners that were taken about Jackson, and among them was one that claimed to be a Parvin. He said that Father and J.A. Parvin of Muscatine were his uncles. And he heard that I was there, and he sent word to me that he wanted to see me. Perhaps Father or Uncle John would know who he was. He enlisted in Texas and the boys said that he was a bitter secessionist. I did not go to see him. Perhaps I done wrong, but I did not want to claim relationship with any man in arms against the laws of his country. I believe that if I had it to do over again, I

---

8. Union General George McClellan ran for President as a Democrat against Abraham Lincoln in 1864 and was defeated 2,203,831 votes to 1,797,019 votes, garnering 45% of the popular vote, but losing 212 votes to 21 votes in the Electoral College. The seceding Confederate states did not participate in this election. B. Catton at 231.

9. Parvin's sentiments that there can be no middle ground in this war echoes the views of Illinois Senator Stephen Douglas who after the surrender of Ft. Sumter said much the same thing to his Illinois constituents: "Every man must be for the United States or against it. There can be no neutrals in this war, only patriots—or traitors." Robert W. Johannsen, "Douglas, Stephen Arnold (1813–1861)," Encyclo. of the Civil War 613, 614.

10. It appears that there were only five Parvins [all from the same nuclear family] who served in Texas regiments in the Civil War. They were: Hosea [the father], and Henry, William, and John [Hosea's sons]—and a second Hosea, possibly Hosea, Jr. Without tracing all the complications involved, it is likely that the Texas Parvin involved in the incident described in Daniel's letter was a distant cousin of Daniel and could have been any one of these Parvins—except for John who was killed in action prior thereto in August 1862. Ancestry.com [1850 Federal census, Pleasant, Fulton County, Texas] ["Hosea Parvin" search]; Ancestry.com, Military search, U.S. Civil War Soldiers 1861–1865, ["Parvin searches"]; C.W. Soldrs. & Sailrs. ["Parvin" searches]; Eleventh Texas Cavalry 1861–65 Website ["Parvin" searches].

should speak to him, for I could of done so without putting me to one bit of trouble. [July 25, 1863: Big Black River near Vicksburg, Miss.]

d. Parvin's Views on Southern Sympathizers in the North

As previously stated, Parvin reserved his most damning invective for the southern sympathizers in the North—the Peace Democrats or "Copperheads" who opposed the war. The following letters are often breathtaking in their bitter condemnations of such people. And the italicized portion of the first letter below has to be the most colorful invective that Parvin ever conjured up.

So you can see something of the character of the men that we have got to fight. They are beings without principle, and the man in the North that will advocate their cause is worse than the devil wants them to be. Yes, they are worse than hell itself. *And if there is a hell, and such men do not get in the hottest spot, why it is a worthless institution, a scarecrow, a humbug, or any other name you have a mind to call it.* [July 17, 1862: Corinth, Miss.]

William,[11] you speak about the Vallandingham[12] democracy. Now I will tell you what I think about him and his followers. As for him, he is an old traitor of the deepest cast. Just such a man as us knows are paid thirteen dollars per month to shoot and if they let me have a shot at him, I will try and waste but one ball on him. And then turn him over to the devil to whom he belongs. And if he had of had him long ago, it would of been a good thing for the country. But I think that his time is about up. And now for his followers. They are either ignorant and deceived or else they are traitors like himself and that being the

---

11. Probably Daniel's brother William S. Parvin. Register of Old Settlers at 130.

12. Parvin is referring to Clement Vallandingham, a member of the U.S. House of Representatives from Ohio (1858–63). He became leader of the Peace Democrats or "Copperheads" who opposed Lincoln's war policies and sought to end the war. He was eventually tried by a military commission and convicted for making public statements against the war and in sympathy with the South. Lincoln later commuted his sentence and banished him to the South. He returned, however, to Canada where he continued his peace agitation, unsuccessfully ran for Governor of Ohio, and helped write the Peace Platform at the 1864 Democratic Convention. B. Catton at 348; Charles F. Howlett, "Vallandingham, Clement Laird (1820–1871)" Encyclo. of the Civil War 2011–13; J.M. McPherson at 591–92, 597.

case, I don't care how soon the devil gets his own. You call them Jeff Davis Democrats and I think that a very good name for them. [August 9–10, 1862: Corinth, Miss.]

Uncle John, you think very much as I do about the traitorous Democrats at the north. If their mouths was once stopped, it would not take the soldiers long to crush out this rebellion. Oh! the traitorous villains, how I hate them. And I should hate to be in their situation expecting to have a hearing before a just God. For terrible will be their punishment, for their crimes are worse than the murders. And I hate them as I should the man that would take the life of his fellow man for gain. [March 30, 1863: Camp below Lake Providence, La.]

Those that die for their country die a noble death. But shame to the traitors and their northern dupes. For above all men they are the meanest. They are a disgrace to the mothers that bore them, a disgrace to the country, and a disgrace to mankind. I am ashamed to be considered a fellow man with any thing so mean. [April 17, 1863: Lake Providence, La.]

Oh! this cruel war, when will it be over and we be allowed to return to our families and friends. But while our country is in trouble, we must try to bear our trials and disappointments with as good a grace as possible and hope for a happy future when this accursed rebellion is put down. This is a very stirring time in this war. Our armies are pressing them hard and they fight desperately causing many a brave man to fall.

And yet some infernal traitors would argue that it is not right to kill the infernal traitors. Oh! how I hate such arguments as that for it tells me that those that utter such sentiments as those are traitors at heart, and I despise treason. [May 25, 1864: Huntsville, Ala.]

Besides Clement Vallandingham whom he despised, Parvin also specifically condemned Edward Thayer [an Iowa Democrat] as being disloyal to the country, and even spoke of lynching him. Thayer was the publisher of a daily newspaper in Muscatine [the Muscatine Daily Courier] and was quite active in the

Democratic Party, both then and later. Thayer ran for Congress as a Democrat in 1862, but was defeated. In 1868 he moved to Clinton, Iowa, and established another newspaper, The Clinton Age, which became an influential Democratic publication.[13]

The following are Parvin's extremely harsh views on Thayer. They begin with Parvin's strong opposition to Thayer's run for Congress in 1862.

> You must beat Thayer if possible for just such men as him and his party has caused all this trouble and are now keeping it up at the present time. And how much longer the Democrat party will continue to dare to hold out encouragements to the traitors, I cannot tell. But if us soldiers were back there, they would have to keep pretty quiet I can assure you. [Aug. 25, 1862: Camp near Bolivar, Tenn.]

> I don't care how soon the devil gets his own. You call them Jeff Davis Democrats and I think that a very good name for them, and Thayer leads that party for Congress. But surely there are enough Union men left at home yet to defeat him. I do not like Butler[14] but he is a thousand times better than Thayer for these times. [Aug. 9, 1862: Corinth, Miss.]

> Parvin,[15] in your letter you speak about Ed. Thare. I have read his papers and I call him a rebel, and I have had about fifty fair shots at better men than he is. And if I were there, I would be willing to be the leader of a squad of ten men that would hitch a rope around his neck and string him up to the first convenient place that we came to. Oh! how I do hate a northern traitor. They are the cause of this war in the first place, and now they are the cause of keeping it a-going. And who-

---

13. B. Gue at 261; L.P. Allen, *The History of Clinton County, Iowa* 693 (Western Historical Co.) (1879).

14. Edward Thayer, however, was defeated for Congress in 1862 by Hiram Price, not by someone named Butler. B. Gue at 261.

15. Parvin is answering a letter from his young nephew William Parvin Freeman, the son of J.P. Freeman [Parvin's business associate in cabinetmaking] and Parvin's sister Lydia. U.S. Census, Muscatine County, Iowa, Household of J.P. Freeman (Sept. 4, 1850). William Parvin Freeman, age 19, subsequently enlisted in the army as a private on January 28, 1864, and was later promoted to second corporal. He mustered out of the army on July 15,1865. Roster & Record, 11th Reg. at 323; C.W. Soldrs. & Sailrs. ["William Freeman" search].

ever says to the contrary is a notorious liar. Why the rebels themselves acknowledge that much. [Feb. 11, 1863: Lake Providence, La.]

_____

And how it is that the loyal people will allow such trash as Thayer to blab treason and yet run at large I cannot see. Yet such is the case. The people and our government deal too mildly with traitors. I wish that such was not the case. [Aug. 6, 1864: Camp near Atlanta, Ga.]

_____

Parvin also castigates as disloyal a member of his regiment who was apparently attempting to run for the Iowa Legislature. Parvin does not name the man, but accuses him of being a part of the Copperheads [or southern sympathizers] whom Parvin despised.

I suppose that there is some hard fighting to do yet, and it is all caused by those infernal Copperheads. But they will have their reward. They are a set of black hearted murderers.

And they are now trying to elect a man from this regiment that tried to get up a band of highwaymen from this regiment only last spring. His idea was to steal all the government property that they could get their hands on, and then strike off for the nearest rebel camp, and get a permit of them to go and kill and plunder as they pleased. And there are any amount of witnesses of these facts here now. They are those that left him when they found out his foul intentions, but he is only a fair specimen of his party.

I did not know of all these things when I was at home. Neither did I know that he was going to be a candidate for office, and especially an office where he will have a vote for U.S. Senator. But I do not think that he will have the chance to vote there. If he does, what can we expect from such a man. It cannot be good to the government. That's so. [Oct. 9, 1863: Vicksburg, Miss.]

_____

In the following letters, Parvin was probably referring to the autumn 1863 state elections in Iowa, when he once again attacked the southern sympathizers in the north [Copperheads], as well as Edward Thayer [the Muscatine newspaperman who was active in the Democratic Party]. Parvin was also highly critical of "Tuttills politics" and was probably referring to the Democratic candidate for Iowa governor, James M. Tuttle, who was actually a brigadier general in the Union Army from Iowa and had fought in the Battle of Shiloh. He was later defeated for governor by the Republican candidate William Milo Stone.[16] Parvin was ultimately pleased with the results of all these elections.

> Now a word to the men folks about the coming election. I have talked with a good many soldiers and they are not a-going to be deceived with regard to Tuttills politics. They say that he is a two-faced man and they will not support any such a man. And I know a good many Democrats that will not support him because he is two-faced. They say that they cannot depend on such a man. [Sept. 20, 1863: Vicksburg, Miss.]

> If the Union ticket prevails this fall, then the war will close this winter. But if the Copperheads prevail, then the war may be prolonged. Oh that accursed party. They are trying to break down the best government that ever was. [Sept. 26, 1863: Vicksburg, Miss.]

> I have not yet heard how the election went, but I have but little fears on that for certainly the good sense of the people will tell them which way to vote. And if they vote right, the war is almost to a close for on this election depends the length of this war. And anybody that is doing any of their own thinking can see this. But if they let such cowardly scamps as Thayer do their thinking, they will be led to the Rebel army—if they are not all like him too cowardly (Oh! the poor trifling pup). [Oct. 25, 1863: Vicksburg, Miss.]

> Well the elections are over and I am glad. Not only that they have gone right, but that the excitement is past, for I always did hate such excitements. [Nov. 8, 1863: Vicksburg, Miss.]

---

16. B. Gue at 269–70.

Section 2. Abraham Lincoln: Emancipation Proclamation, Black Union Regiments, and Call for More Troops

Although not terribly enthusiastic, Parvin favored Abraham Lincoln for re-election to the presidency in 1864 over the Democrat George McClellan, whom Parvin despised as a traitor. [See Oct. 15, 1864 letter, quoted in Section 1c supra] Later, however, Parvin warmed more to his decision to support Lincoln.

As for Lincoln's Emancipation Proclamation and his decision to create black Union regiments, Parvin was strongly in favor. Although probably not a believer in racial equality,[17] he thought that freeing the slaves and creating black Union regiments would help win the war and preserve the Union. Parvin also approved of Lincoln's calling up more troops in June 1862.

> Wm,[18] I have thought some on what you wrote to me about. And I am willing to admit that Lincoln is not my first choice for president, but he is better than a Copperhead and if he is nominated I expect that I shall support him. [June 16, 1864: Camp 11th Iowa, Atlanta campaign]

> William, I guess that Old Abe is the man for everyone to support that wishes his country's welfare.[19] [June 29, 1864: Camp 11th Iowa, Atlanta campaign]

> William, your way of thinking and mine are nearly alike as regards slavery. If we cannot have the Union with it, let's have the Union without

---

17. As an aside, in one letter Parvin indicates that he might get a promotion to corporal if he agreed to serve in a black regiment, but states that his wife would not want him to do that. [May 9, 1864: Clifton, Tenn.] This reference, as well as others in which Parvin refers to black soldiers as "darkies," probably indicates the prevailing white prejudice against African-Americans of that day.

18. In this letter and the next two letters, it is likely that Parvin is replying to a letter from his brother William S. Parvin. William is one of Parvin's more frequent correspondents. Register of Old Settlers at 130.

19. As it turned out, Lincoln carried about 78% of the soldiers' vote out of the some 150,000 soldier ballots cast in the presidential election of 1864. Adam I.P. Smith, "Soldiers' Votes," Encyclo. of the Civil War at 1823.

it. The President's Proclamation[20] suits me very well. Only it had ought
to of come a year earlier. [Oct. 15–16, 1862: Camp near Corinth, Miss.]

Sarah, there are good prospects of this rebellion being crushed out
now, for our government are organizing and arming the negroes and
telling them to fight for their freedom. And there are several regiments
now full and a good many more fast filling up. And I and most all the
soldiers say amen to them. And amen to the administration for adopt-
ing this policy, and it had ought to of been done long ago. But it is better late than not at all. But if they had of done it a year and a half ago,
it would of saved a great many lives and an immense amount of property.[21] [April 7, 1863: Camp near Lake Providence, La.]

I am in hopes that this dreadful war is nearly over. Or in other words,
I am in hopes that the rebels are nearly subdued for I want peace on
no other terms. And the negroes are now free and they (I mean the government) are arming them and putting white men over them to lead
them on to victory and their freedom. And this must make the traitors tremble, for this is turning their support against them and it is bound
to give them their death stroke. [April 17, 1863: Lake Providence, La.]

Day before yesterday the rebels and darkies had a nice little fight about
ten miles above this place. The numbers were about equal, but the
rebels had the advantage for they had artillery and the darkies had

---

20. Lincoln's Emancipation Proclamation was announced on September 22, 1862, and
took effect January 1, 1863, freeing all slaves held in states and portions of states still in rebellion. B. Catton at 105.

21. One historical authority outlines the participation of African-American troops in the
Union army:

> Of the 178,975 "Colored Troops" that served in the Union army, 99,337 were re-
> cruited in the South, thus diminishing Southern resources because most blacks
> were engaged in agricultural pursuits. Black troops made up nearly 12 percent of
> the Union army in service in 1864 and 1865, and could be justly proud of their
> record. One in three were casualties. They served in 449 engagements, including
> thirty-nine major battles. They were organized into 120 regiments of infantry,
> seven of cavalry, twelve of heavy artillery, and ten batteries of light artillery.

Duane C. Young, "Army, United States" Encyclo. of the Civil War 110, 111.

none. And after a severe fight, the darkies charged on them, taking 200 prisoners and five pieces of artillery. The loss is said to be severe on both sides. I say bully for the darky. They deserve their freedom and they shall have it, the Copperheads notwithstanding. [June 9, 1863: Camp near Vicksburg, Miss.]

Sarah, in your letter of the first, you ask me what I think of the President in calling out more troops. I look at it as a precautionary move against [the] possibility of triumph on the part of the rebels. I think that the rebellion is nearly put down unless the enemy should gain some decided victory over our troops. And the President in calling for more men is guarding against that. [June 14, 1862: Camp near Corinth, Miss.]

Section 3. General Ulysses S. Grant and Other Civil War Generals

Parvin held an extremely low opinion of General Ulysses S. Grant after the Battle of Shiloh [April 6–7, 1862]—and even questioned Grant's loyalty to the country. He did not see Grant on the field of battle, incorrectly thought Grant was asleep in the nearby town of Savannah, Tennessee, and no doubt blamed Grant for being taken by surprise with a Confederate attack on the first day of the conflict. The fact that Grant rallied his forces the second day and drove the Confederates from the field to claim a Union victory, did not change Parvin's opinion.

Later, however, Parvin did an about-face on Grant without taking back his earlier harsh attacks. During the Battle of Vicksburg in which he participated, Parvin stated that the soldiers "placed a good deal of confidence" in Grant, and that the latter "will do this thing up about right." [June 16, 1863: Camp near Vicksburg, Miss.]

Thereafter, Grant won this battle when Vicksburg fell on July 4, 1863, giving the Union complete control of the Mississippi River and splitting the Confederacy in two. Apparently, Parvin was impressed with Grant's plan of attack on Vicksburg, which later proved both successful and [according to Grant's Memoirs] the turning point of the Civil War.[22]

---

22. U.S. Grant, *Personal Memoirs of U.S. Grant* 352 (orig. ed. 1885) (Barnes & Noble paperback ed.) (2003).

What follows are Parvin's early harsh evaluations of Grant.

We had no General at all [referring to the Battle of Shiloh, April 6–7, 1862]. General Grant, it is said, was at Savannah asleep. One thing is certain: he was not with his command. I have no confidence in the man. If General Buell had of been in command on Sunday they would not of drove us back as they did. [April 14, 1862: Pittsburg Landing, Tenn.]

———————

Well, I have just been out to the regiment, and when out there, I heard bad news. In the first place, I heard that General Grant was in command of this army. He is the same man that was in command at the Battle of Shiloh, and he done his best then to have this army destroyed. And I do not believe that he is too good to sell his army and deliver them into the hands of the rebels. So you must be prepared to hear anything: either that we are all killed or all taken prisoners or anything else that is in his power that will benefit the enemy of our country. It makes me mad to see how things are worked sometimes. [July 17, 1862: Corinth, Miss.]

At Vicksburg, however, Parvin softened his views and gave Grant a vote of confidence—although expressing no regret for his earlier negative opinions.

The affairs about Vicksburg are as near as I can judge about as they were when I last wrote. We are still here watching them and they are in town watching us. And so the matter stands. They are expecting re-inforcements to come up behind us, and we are looking for them too. And we are a-getting ready to meet them when they come, and if they cannot bring more than forty or fifty thousand, they had better stay away—for we can whip that many and hold these fellows in town at the same time. At least we think so.

And Genl. Grant does not seem to be alarmed about them, and we all place a good deal of confidence in him. And I think that he will do this thing up about right. But time will tell, and we must have a little patience. [June 16, 1863: Vicksburg, Miss.]

———————

Parvin also expresses opinions on other Union and Confederate generals of the day. In particular, he has high praise for both Union General Don Carlos Buell and Confederate General Pierre Beauregard for their respective parts in the Battle of Shiloh:

If General Buell[23] had of been in command on Sunday [during the Shiloh battle], they would not of drove us back as they did. Buell got here Sunday evening and he sent out word along the lines that if we would keep them in check two hours longer, he would take them off of our hands and let us rest. And from that time we commenced to drive them back. When we had drove them back about half a mile, night came on and fighting was nearly stopped for the night. And early next morning the firing was commenced (Buell being as good as his word), and he commenced to drive them, and we kept driving them all day until almost night and then they broke and run. [April 14, 1862: Pittsburg Landing, Tenn.]

——————

They [the Confederates] have quite a large army yet and they are brave men. And Beauregard [Confederate general] is a very good general. It is very easy to see the effect of a good general on a battlefield. And Beauregard proved himself such here on Sunday. The men under him fought with desperation. * * * I do know that they fought like brave men. And I could see by their movements that they were drilled a great deal better than we were, for they went through some maneuvers on the battlefield right under fire that we cannot do right on the drill ground, much less the battlefield. [April 14, 1862: Pittsburg Landing, Tenn.]

——————

Parvin also placed complete confidence in Union General Henry Halleck, who took command of Union forces after the Battle of Shiloh and proceeded at a glacial pace in pursuit of General Beauregard and the Confederate forces to Corinth, Tennessee—allowing such forces to escape.

General Halleck is in command in person here now, and I do not think that he will carry on a battle as the one was carried on here on

———————

23. General Don Carlos Buell joined Grant on the second day of the Shiloh Battle with 25,000 additional troops and helped preserve a Union victory. D.J. Eicher at 229–30. A West Point graduate, General Buell served with distinction in the Mexican War and was in command of the Army of the Ohio at the time of Shiloh. He participated in a number of battles in the western theater of the Civil War, but, like McClellan, was eventually replaced by Lincoln for pursing the Confederate forces too slowly. Stephen D. Engle, "Buell, Don Carlos," Encyclo. of Civil War 308–09.

the sixth. If he does, they may whip us out of here yet. But I have no fears of that for I put full confidence in our general, and I think that he will fetch us through all right. [April 23, 1862: Pittsburg Landing, Tenn.]

―――――――

You will learn from the papers that General Halleck is advancing the army on Corinth with great caution. And the regiment that I am in is said to be within two and a half miles of Corinth. So you see that he is a-getting us up middling close. How much closer they will allow us to come and fortify I do not know, but I should think not much. [May 18, 1862: Camp near Corinth, Miss.]

―――――――

We (that is, our division) are encamped in the same place that we were when I wrote last. We have a good breastwork here and the boys all think that if the enemy were to attack us here, we could whip them three to one. But I do not think that there is any probability of them attacking us here. And I think that if they wait for General Halleck to attack them, it will be several days yet, but I do not pretend to know. But I put full confidence in him, and I am perfectly willing to wait on him until he thinks that he is ready. And then he will pitch in without my advice. [May 26, 1862: Camp near Corinth, Miss.]

―――――――

In the Union advance on Corinth, Mississippi, Parvin favorably mentions General Buell's attack on the Confederate forces:

We are now within about ten miles of Corinth and they say eight miles from the enemy. Last night a part of Gen. Buell's forces attacked one wing of their forces and drove them back and captured a considerable number of prisoners. I cannot say how many, for there is various reports. And I expect that if it had not of rained today, the attack would of been followed up today. [May 4, 1862: Buena Vista, Miss.][24]

―――――――

24. As an aside, Parvin also mentions several other Union and Confederate generals in narrating his travels in the war theater. After the fall of Atlanta, Georgia, on September 2, 1864, Parvin writes that General William T. Sherman was fortifying Atlanta and that Confederate General John Bell Hood was unlikely to drive Sherman from the city. [October 19,

Section 4. Assessment of Fellow Soldiers

Parvin liked his fellow soldiers and thought well of them on the whole. He may have also felt a certain bonding with them as a combat unit—the way most soldiers in most wars feel about the soldiers with whom they fight. But he never writes about this in his letters.

Company C and company H are both quartered in the same room which makes us about as thick as bees. But the boys are generally good-natured, and so we get along with but very little trouble. [Nov. 26, 1861: Benton Barracks, St. Louis, Mo.]

If I was there, I could tell you some good jokes on some of the boys and some pretty hard stories on the others, but I shall keep them off the paper. I could tell you some things that the boys would not have told on them for anything. And so the world goes on, and I am here in the army studying human nature and nature itself. I am sometimes pleased with the study; at other times disgusted. But take it all together, I am rather pleased than otherwise. There are some strange beings in this world in the form of man. [Jan. 14–16, 1862: California, Mo.]

Last night there was a good many of the boys drunk, and I do not except the officers, for I believe that they were worse than the men. Oh! this thing of soldiering; it will ruin many a good boy. [Jan. 17, 1863: Memphis, Tenn.]

Section 5. Views on the Length of the War

Parvin held generally a pessimistic view on whether the war would end soon. He thought it could go on for years—even estimating as long as ten years.

This war will last just as long as the lawmakers at Washington continue inactive, and in my opinion if they do not wake up pretty soon, it will be too late to save our government from divisions and de-

---

1864: Atlanta, Ga.] He also refers in passing to Union General George Thomas and Confederate General Nathan Bedford Forrest. [Nov. 8, 1863: Vicksburg, Miss.] [May 9, 1864: Clifton, Tenn.]

struction. But these are gloomy thoughts, and I try to keep them from my mind as much as I can. But in spite of myself they will occasionally come across my mind. [Jan. 28, 1862: California, Mo.]

———————

Sarah, you want me to give my opinion about the length of this war. Now I don't want you to consider my opinion in this of much account, but I fear that this war will last for the next ten years yet. I could give you my reasons for believing as I do (for you know that I always have a reason for my belief), but I am in hopes that I am mistaken in this. I hope that we will discharged in the spring. [Feb. 3, 1862: California, Mo.]

———————

I think now that the prospect for the war ending this winter is good. But it is impossible for me to see into the future. [Oct. 21, 1862: Camp near Corinth, Miss.]

———————

I do not feel in as good spirits about the war's closing now as I did when I wrote my last letter. But it is something that I cannot tell anything about, and the less I think and bother myself about it, the better I am off. [Oct. 28, 1862: Camp near Corinth, Miss.]

———————

I hope the war will be ended by the time you think. And I think it all depends almost entirely on the eastern army if they are successful. But if they get whipped there, then we cannot look for peace for some time to come. [Dec. 7, 1862: Camp near Abbeville, Miss.]

———————

Sarah, you ask me if I think that the war will last three years. That I don't know. But if it does, I want you to be ready to leave the country with me as soon as my time is up, for I think that will be the best thing that I can do. And I should like to know whether you are willing to go with me or not. I think that some place in Brazil will suit me. [Feb. 11, 1863: Lake Providence, La.]

———————

You want me to give my opinion about the war closing by the first of Jan. I do not think it will close so soon as that. [Aug. 12, 1864: Camp near Atlanta, Ga.]

Abraham Lincoln

Parvin was initially unenthusiastic in his support for Lincoln in the presidential election of 1864, stating that Lincoln was "not my first choice." Later, however, Parvin warmed to the idea, stating that everyone who wished his country well should support "Old Abe."

Courtesy of the Library of Congress, Civil War Collection.

Union General George McClellan

Commander of all Union forces in the early part of the Civil War and, later, Lincoln's Democratic opponent in the presidential election of 1864. Parvin hated McClellan and "all those that would try to ruin their country by voting for him."

Courtesy of the Library of Congress, Civil War Collection.

Union General Ulysses S. Grant

Parvin initially had "no confidence" in Grant's leadership at the Battle of Shiloh, accusing Grant of being absent from the battle and conducting himself as a near-traitor. Later, however, Parvin changed his mind about Grant during the Vicksburg campaign, stating "we all place a good deal of confidence in him."

Courtesy of the Library of Congress, Civil War Collection.

Union General Don Carlos Buell

Parvin had high praise for General Buell's performance at the Battle of Shiloh, stating that Buell was "as good as his word" when the latter arrived with additional troops on the second day of the Shiloh Battle and helped secure a Union victory.

Courtesy of the Library of Congress, Civil War Collection.

Union General Henry Halleck

Parvin "put full confidence" in General Halleck after the latter took command of Union troops following the Shiloh Battle, although Halleck proceeded at a glacial pace to Corinth, Mississippi, allowing Confederate troops to escape.

Courtesy of the Library of Congress, Civil War Collection.

Confederate General Pierre Beauregard

Parvin thought that General Beauregard was a "very good" commander at the Battle of Shiloh, stating that his men "fought with desperation" and were "drilled a good deal better" than the Union troops.

Courtesy of the Library of Congress, Civil War Collection.

Union General William T. Sherman

Parvin's top commander in the 1864 Atlanta campaign.
Courtesy of the Library of Congress, Civil War collection.

Chapter 4

Army Camp Life

The letters in this chapter give an account of Parvin's everyday experience in the various places where he and his regiment were encamped during his entire army service. They give a reasonably accurate picture of what the average Union private experienced on a regular basis during the Civil War.

Section 1. Reckless Weapons Handling

Before launching into these routine camp activities, however, two shocking incidents occurred in Parvin's early camp life that were anything but routine. Both are recounted below. In each instance, young and inexperienced recruits recklessly mishandled their weapons with disastrous results, one resulting in a ghastly death.

> Yesterday two of the Iowa Third [Regiment] boys got to fooling with their guns, pointing them at each other and snapping them. And one of the guns went off tearing the whole top of the other's head off, scattering his brains for twenty feet. He died in about ten minutes. I fear some of such accidents in our company when we get our guns loaded, for some of the boys are very careless. [Dec. 2, 1861: St. Louis at Benton Barracks]

> Night before last, one of the men of Company K shot one of his hands. He was on guard and got to fooling with his gun, and put his right hand over the muzzle, and let a stick of wood fall on the hammer, knocking the gun off and taking two fingers with it. There is so much carelessness in the army that it is a great wonder to me that there is not more accidents than there is. [Jan. 14, 1862: California, Mo.]

Section 2. Letters

Turning now to more every-day activities, a vital part of Parvin's camp life was receiving letters from home and answering them. Like any soldier in any war, Parvin was often very lonely and craved letters from home. In response to his constant pleas, Parvin regularly received letters from his wife, relatives and friends during his entire army service. As he wrote later, "nothing cheers the soldier like having news from home." [May 18, 1862: Camp near Corinth, Miss.]

Parvin answered these letters by replying in a single omnibus letter, as he had no time to individually answer every piece of correspondence he received. He often wrote these letters under trying circumstances, such as poor light, constant barracks noise, crowded conditions, frequent interruptions and poor writing surfaces. And he sometimes wrote a single letter over a period of two or more days and dated it accordingly. Moreover, the paper on which he wrote his correspondence was sometimes soiled due to various conditions of army life.

a. Pleas for Letters

Parvin's pleas for letters from home are constant throughout most of his army service. And when those requested letters failed to show up, he was very depressed. Indeed, his homesickness during his first Christmas away from home with no letters is particularly touching. That letter is italicized below.

I hope that you will write as often as once a week. [Nov. 10, 1861: Camp McClellan, Davenport, Iowa]

Sarah, I want you to write often and I want you to tell all our folks to write to me, as news from home will be very acceptable to me. [Nov. 20, 1861: Benton Barracks, St. Louis, Mo.]

Sarah, this is a lonesome world to me without you are with me, and I miss Fred Andy [his son] very much. Kiss him for me and tell all my relatives and friends to write me. And don't forget to write often yourself, for letters from home will be very cheering to me. [Nov. 26, 1861: St. Louis, Mo.]

I have not got a letter yet and nearly all the boys have got letters and it makes me feel bad to think that I do not get any. But I am satisfied that there is a good reason. If I thought that I was neglected by my friends, I should feel worse than I do.

I had to go and drill yesterday and did not have time to finish this and I am glad that I did not for when I came in, there was a letter for me. And it made me feel glad to hear from you, and so this morning I am feeling very well. But I only got one letter. I thought that I ought to of had three or four. * * *

If you want me to keep in good spirits, don't forget to write often. Tell Father, Mother, Ella, Hannah, Jane, Josiah, Laura, William, Lizza, Freeman Parvin[1] and a whole host of others that I have not room to put down. [Dec. 2–3, 1861: Benton Barracks, St. Louis, Mo.]

Sarah, do write as often as you can. It makes me feel so lonesome when the mail comes and I do not get a letter. [Dec. 9–10, 1861: Jefferson City, Mo.]

Christmas was a dreadful long and lonesome day to me. I am in hopes that you enjoyed yourselves better than I did. Oh! how I long for home. I would willingly give a month's wages to be a week with those that I love.

* * * Another mail has come and no letters for me. It makes me feel almost forsaken for the rest of the boys to get letters and me receive none. [Dec. 28–30, 1861: California, Mo.]

---

1. In this group of family members, Parvin is referring to his father William Parvin, and his mother Hannah Parvin. He is also most likely referring to his brothers Josiah Parvin and William S. Parvin, as well as his sister Elizabeth Purcell. As for his reference to Parvin, this would be his nephew William Parvin Freeman [the son of Parvin's sister Lydia and his business associate J.P. Freeman]. Register of Old Settlers at 130; 1850 U.S. Census, Muscatine, Iowa, Household of J.P. Freeman, Ancestry.com. The rest, however, have not been identified.

As an aside, William Parvin Freeman, age 19, subsequently enlisted in the army as a private on January 28, 1864, and was later promoted to second corporal. He mustered out of the army on July 15,1865. Roster & Record, 11th Reg. at 323; C.W. Soldrs. & Sailrs. ["William Freeman" search].

I don't want you to forget to write me long letters. I will try and find time to read them two or three times over. [July 13, 1862: Corinth, Miss.]

Sarah, you say in your letter of the 13th that you missed writing to me the week before because you did not get a letter from me. Now that was not right for to keep me on suspense because you did not get your letters. Now suppose that I was to adopt the same plan. We would soon stop writing altogether. Now I have not had a letter from you for over three weeks. And still I kept on writing just the same, and that is once a week. And I want you to keep on writing to me even if you should not get a letter from me for a few weeks. But I will try and write every week. But something might turn up that I could not write. But if I do not write, I will try and have a good excuse. [July 27, 1862: Corinth, Miss.]

Sarah, since I last wrote, I have only received one letter, and that was from you. And I feel very thankful that you write so often for it tells me that I am not forgotten at home. And I feel especially proud of my last letter for it was a big full one. And I read it with a great deal of interest. You say that you are afraid that I will be bothered to read your letter. If you write as good as you can, I shall not be bothered to read your letters. So you need not give yourself any uneasiness about that, but write big letters every time and I will manage to read them. [Nov. 17, 1862: Grand Junction, Tenn.]

I have not received a letter from home for over two weeks, and it is no wonder that I cannot think of anything to write for I have almost got the blues. Now I am satisfied that you do not neglect me, but I feel so lonesome when I do not get my letters regular. I think that there will be a mail in today, for the newsboys are here with late papers. And how disappointed I shall be if I get no letter. [Oct. 4, 1863: Vicksburg, Miss.]

Well Sarah, I have not had a letter from you for about three weeks. What is the matter? Have you forgotten how I look? If that is so, I shall have to try and leave my likeness with you next time. Or maybe

I did this time, and that's what's the matter. I am uneasy all the time about you, and I want you to write regular if you can. And perhaps you do and I have not got them yet. I think that is the most likely way. [Oct. 17, 1863: Big Black River, Vicksburg, Miss.]

b. Omnibus Answer Letters

Parvin frequently wrote omnibus letters to his wife, relatives and friends—in which he responded to everyone in a single letter. He did this because he had no time to individually answer every letter he received, and besides it would be too costly for him to buy the paper and stamps needed for individual letters.

I want my friends all to write to me, and I will acknowledge the receipt of them in letters that I write to you. They cannot expect me to answer every letter. My time will not admit of it. I want you to show them my letters, and I think that will satisfy them. [Dec. 6, 1861: Benton Barracks, St. Louis, Mo.]

———————

I want you all to consider this an answer to your letters, and I want you all to write again. You will see the inconsistency of my answering all of your letters separate. In the first place, it would take more time than I have. And in the second place, I would have no news to write, and it would cost a good deal to send so many letters. Now I want you all to write as often as you can for I am always glad to hear from home. [Dec. 19, 1861: Jefferson City, Mo.]

c. Homesickness

Parvin was an emotional man. A heart-wrenching homesickness and loneliness permeate his letters throughout his long army service. That is why he craved letters from home so much, as they gave him great comfort. Once again, his Christmas letter—this one in 1863—is poignant and is italicized below.

The great trouble with me is to be separated from my family and friends which I can assure you is a great trial to me. But as it cannot be helped for the present, I shall have to try and bear it as well as I can. [March 30, 1862: Pittsburg Landing, Tenn.]

———————

One thing I do know and that is that I am tired of fighting and tired of soldiering in any shape. The fact is I am homesick, yes very homesick, and yet I cannot get there now. If I had of been one of the lucky ones in the fight and got wounded or if I had of got scared and run so hard as to strain myself, then I might of had a chance to come home. The first way is honorable, but I despise the men that adopted the other plan. [April 23, 1862: Pittsburg Landing, Tenn.]

Sarah you say that you have the blues enough for both of us. Well now, I don't see that your having the blues helps me any. For I have them about so much anyhow, and that is about all the time, except when I think that there is a good prospect of my getting home pretty soon. I have now been in the service a little over a year, and a long year it has been to me, and the idea of having to stay two years longer is dreadful. But I try and not think of such things any more than I can help. [Oct. 21, 1862: Camp near Corinth, Miss.]

I need a good deal of cheering up whilst I am soldiering for it is a very dreary business to me. And the longer I follow it, the worse I hate it. [Jan. 26, 1863: Camp near Vicksburg, Miss.]

I have been very homesick for three or four days past, and I am not entirely over it yet. [Feb. 3, 1863: Opposite the mouth of the Yazoo River, near Vicksburg, Miss.]

Sarah, you seem to want to see me very bad. But I do not think that you want to see [me] any worse than I want to see you. I want to see you so bad that I am almost homesick and have got the blues. But all this does no good, and I shall have to content myself the best I can, for it does no good to complain. [July 25, 1863: Big Black River near Jackson, Miss.]

Sarah, I am very lonesome today. If I could only see you and talk with you an hour, it would do me so much good. But that cannot be for the present. But I live in hopes of a better day a-coming. [Nov. 14, 1863: Vicksburg, Miss.]

————————

Tomorrow is Christmas and the thought of home and the pleasant times there will make it a gloomy day to me. But I do not envy anybody in their enjoyment. I only wish that I was in the situation to enjoy myself along with the rest. Tomorrow will be the third Christmas that I have spent in the service of my country and Oh! what a long time it has been to me. [Dec. 24, 1863: Vicksburg, Miss.]

d. Difficulties in Writing Letters in Camp

Parvin encountered a number of physical and other difficulties in writing letters home in camp. Here are a few examples.

It is but little use for me to attempt to write here. Just imagine yourself in a room with from fifty to seventy men and all trying to make as much noise as he can, and then you can have something of an idea of the place that I am in now. * * * It seems to me that it has been a long time since I saw you [Sarah, his wife], but when I reckon the time, it has been only one month. But to me it has been a dreadful long one. * * * I am writing this sitting on my bunk and writing on my knee with no lapboard but my pocket book, and I am getting tired of setting and nothing of importance to write. And if there was in this confusion, I could not think of it. [Nov. 10, 1861: Camp McClellan, Davenport, Iowa]

————————

I do not know whether I shall be able to finish tonight for it is nearly dark now, and I do not know whether I can get a piece of a candle or not. If I can, I will finish. I have [now] got a piece of a candle, and so I will try and keep my word. [Dec. 9, 1861: Jefferson City, Mo.]

————————

I cannot get to write very long at a time. And I am all the time being disturbed by men running against me and shoving around. So I have but little chance to write at all, but I try to do the best that I can under the circumstances. [January 14–16, 1862: California, Mo.]

————————

Since I commenced to write this, I been called off three or four times to drill and do other things that has to be done about camp. The fact is I have a very poor chance to write, and I will be called off in a few moments to drill again. But such is a soldier's life. [April 23–24, 1862: Pittsburg Landing, Tenn.]

As I have a little spare time this afternoon, I thought that I would improve it by writing to you. And I do not know how long it will be before I shall have another spare time, for I am on duty nearly all the time. And when I am on duty, I have no time to write. So I have to take the time that I have, and this makes two letters that I have written this week. And I intend to write as often as I can. And Sarah I do not want you to get low-spirited if you do not get a letter from me every week, for sometimes I am situated so that I cannot write every week. And I do not want you to think that I neglect you. And when I do write, you do not always get my letters regular. [Oct. 28, 1863: Vicksburg, Miss.]

Sarah, I feel very low-spirited today. My thoughts are with you but in person I am a long way off. If I were there I might be happy. Sarah, my thoughts are so unsettled that I shall have to stop writing and finish some other day. [Dec. 2, 1863: Vicksburg, Miss.]

e. Condition of Parvin's Letter Paper

Parvin's letter paper was at times soiled due to various conditions he encountered in camp. The paper itself, however, was extremely durable as the letters have survived intact, although written nearly a century and a half ago.

I suppose that you will wonder how this paper got so dirty. Well I will tell you. I had the ink bottle in my knapsack with the rest of my things and it got broke. And my paper is not the only thing that got dobbed up with it, but nearly everything that I have got dobbed over with ink. [May 14, 1863: Grand Gulf, Miss.]

Sarah, you may think that this is a pretty hard-looking sheet of paper to write a letter on. But consider that I carried it with me on the tramp and the weather [is] about as hot as it gets; and the dust about shoe-mouth deep a part of the way; and it rained and the things that was not wet with sweat mostly got wet with rain. So taking all things into consideration, I think that it looks very well and I have lots more just like it; and as long as it lasts I do not think of buying any more. [June 1, 1863: Haines Bluffs, Miss.]

f. Interruptions in Army Mail Service

Parvin was upset when he was temporarily cut off from mail service on three occasions—one because of the alleged negligence of an army functionary, another stemming from an interruption in rail service, and the last while he was aboard a steamship en route to the Battle of Shiloh. It is amazing, how-ever, that the mail service otherwise operated with considerable efficiency dur-ing Parvin's entire army service.

Since I wrote to you, I have not received any letters, but I do not think that the fault is yours. I think the trouble is in our regimental preast[?]. He will not send the mail until he gets a list of the sick that were left there. Now you see that he would rather keep back our let-ters rather than go to the hospital and get a list for himself. The lazy cuss. He is a-drawing pay from the government and what good does he do? I am sure that I cannot see what. I do not want to wish him any great harm, but I do wish that he was in heaven with his head off so that he would not trouble us any more. [Dec. 28, 1861: Cali-fornia, Mo.]

The [railroad] cars ran off the track yesterday about ten miles below here and, in consequence of that, we had no mail last night. And I am in hopes of getting a letter when the cars come in today. [Febru-ary 26–27, 1862: California, Mo.]

There is one thing that is very disagreeable to some of us. And that is that we have got beyond all regular mail. We cannot send letters; nei-ther will we get our letters regular. [March 15, 1862: On board the steamer "Southwestern" en route to the Battle of Shiloh, Pittsburg Landing, Tenn.]

g. Parvin's Letter Journal

Parvin kept a journal that recorded the dates of the letters he wrote home. That journal, however, has long since been lost. Indeed, all the letters that Parvin received from home during the War have also been lost.

> Sarah, when you answer my letters, I wish you would give the date of the letter (or letters) that you are answering. And then I shall know whether you get all of my letter[s] or not, for I keep a journal of when I write. [July 13, 1862: Corinth, Miss.]

h. Day-to-day Correspondence

Many of the letters are taken up with mundane and sometimes obscure matters as Parvin responded to his many family correspondents in single omnibus letters. Here is a sampling of these many everyday references.

> Laura, I thank you for your invitation to help you eat a turkey on Christmas. I guess that I shall not be there so soon, but I will try and think about it on Christmas about dinner time and that will have to do me.
>
> Tillie, you say that you are in a writing humor pretty often. You say that you missed me at Father's at the dinner table. Well I think very likely you did. I should of liked to of been there. You say that you and Sarah could not eat for thinking about me. Well that was too bad, but I can't help your thoughts.
>
> Mother, you say you know that I have not forgotten you although I have not written to you. No, I have not forgotten any of my friends and especially my Mother. Now Mother, I consider that I have written to you all. You cannot expect me to direct a letter to all of you. If I was to do that, I should have to neglect my wife and that I can't do, neither do I believe that you want me to.
>
> Parvin,[2] you want me to tell you who it was that we all turned out to see at St. Louis. I cannot tell you for I do not know. [Dec. 19, 1861: Jefferson City, Mo.]

---

2. Parvin is answering a letter from his young nephew William Parvin Freeman, the son of J.P. Freeman [Parvin's business associate] and Parvin's sister Lydia. 1850 U.S. Census, Muscatine, Iowa, Household of J.P. Freeman, Ancestry.com. William Parvin Freeman, age 19, subsequently enlisted in the army as a private on January 28, 1864, and was later promoted to second corporal. He mustered out of the army on July 15, 1865. Roster & Record, 11th Reg. at 323; C.W. Soldrs. & Sailrs. ["William Freeman" search].

Father, you say that crops do not look very well and that your corn did not come up well, for all of which I feel sorry. * * * Mother, I have to thank you for your good advice to me, and I shall try and do pretty nearly right so far as my judgment teaches me. * * * Sarah, you speak about having your hair cut off. Now I think that long hair becomes a woman the best, but you can do as you have a mind to about cutting it off. [June 26, 1862: Corinth, Miss.]

Aunt Mary, I am truly thankful that you wrote to me, and I am thankful that you think so much of my family. It gives me great consolation to know that they have such a good place to stay whilst I am away trying to serve my country. For if those that I love most dear had no good place to stay whilst I am gone, it would grieve me almost to death. But owing to your and Uncle's goodness, I feel pretty easy on that point now [Jan. 26, 1863: Camp near Vicksburg, Miss.]

Josiah,[3] I am sorry that the shop that you leased is turning out to you no better, but I am in hopes that it will turn out well to you yet. Yes, Laura I am always glad to get a letter from any of you. [January 25, 1864: Vicksburg, Miss.]

Section 3. Camp Illnesses

Because of the often unsanitary conditions of the camps, the physical exertion of army service, the often poor diet, the lack of adequate medical care, and the sometimes freezing or excessively hot weather, Parvin and other soldiers were frequently sick, often seriously so. This was a pervasive experience for Parvin throughout his army service.[4]

---

3. Parvin is likely answering a letter from his brother Josiah Parvin. Old Settlers Register at 130; 1850 U.S. Census, Muscatine, Iowa, Household of J.P. Freeman, Ancestry.com.

4. A comprehensive study of soldier deaths in the Civil War concludes that disease was by far the most common cause of soldier fatalities:

Twice as many Civil War soldiers died of disease as of battle wounds. The war, Union surgeon general William A. Hammond later observed, was fought at the "end of the medical middle ages." Neither the germ theory nor the nature and

Soon after he arrived in St. Louis for basic training, Parvin came down with sick headaches that plagued him for the remainder of his army service. And later he had a terrible bout of near-pneumonia after standing guard in freezing temperatures—as well as another bout of malarial fever after becoming overheated while removing tree stumps in hot weather.

In April 1862, after escaping near-death at the Battle of Shiloh, Parvin wrote: "I have been sick more since I have been a soldier than I was in all my life before put together." [April 14, 1862: Pittsburg Landing, Tenn.] And he was 35 when he enlisted.

a. Sick Headache

The illness that Parvin was most plagued with throughout his army service was a chronic sick headache. Often the pain was severe and caused him to vomit. For the most part, however, he simply put up with it and went about his army duties in a weakened condition. Other times, the pain was so bad that he had to report sick.

> You [his wife Sarah] want to know whether I have my health. I have not been sick only one night and [a] day since I left Muscatine, and that was on new years night and new years. I had the sick headache, and I was on guard that night, and I vomited until I strained my breast so that I did not get over it for two days. After my turn on guard was out, I went to my bunk and laid there all day new years. And nobody came to me to ask how I was or put their hand on my forehead. I

---

necessity of antisepsis was yet understood. A wave of epidemic disease—measles, mumps, and smallpox—swept through the armies of volunteers in the early months of the war, then yielded precedence to the intractable camp illnesses: diarrhea and dysentery, typhoid and malaria. Nearly three-quarters of Union soldiers suffered from serious bowel complaints in every year of the war; by 1865 the sick rate for diarrhea and dysentery was 995 per thousand. Contamination of water supply from camp latrines was a key cause of these illnesses, as it was of typhoid.

Drew Gilpin Faust, *This Republic of Suffering: Death and the American Civil War* 4 (Alfred A. Knopf publisher) (2008).

Another historical authority gives more particular statistics:

During the Civil War, three of every five Union soldiers who died did so from disease. For the Confederacy two of every three deaths resulted from disease. Roughly 224,000 Union officers and soldiers died of disease, while such ailments claimed about 164,000 Confederates.

Matthew Pacer, "Disease," Encyclo. of the Civil War at 603.

could not help thinking how different it would be if I was at home. [Jan. 7, 1862: California, Mo.]

Your [Sarah's] letter yesterday found me sick and in bed. One of the boys handed it to me, and I did not know whether I could get up and read it or no. But I did stay up long enough to read it. And then I went to bed again, and this morning I was a good deal better. And now it is after noon and I am well or nearly so. The trouble was the sick headache.

Sarah, you say that you think that a soldiers life is a hard life at the best. You are right, it is, and especially for me. If it was not for you, it would suit me better. But I do not think that I was intended for a soldier. But I am into it now and have to stand it. [Jan. 23, 1862: California, Mo.]

I should of wrote two or three days ago but my duties prevented me, and yesterday I was sick. I had a middling hard spell of the sick headache. I had to lay in my bunk all day, and today my head feels somewhat clumsy. It made me shed tears yesterday to think that I was laying here sick and those that I love were far from me. But such is a soldier's life, and I shall have to stand my turn of guard tonight. [Feb. 12, 1862: California, Mo.]

Since I have been on the boat, I have been sick one day with the sick headache. But with the exception of that, I have been well. But it is a wonder to me that we ain't nearly all sick; the way we live is enough to make anybody sick. We have nothing but raw bacon, hard crackers and coffee. [March 15, 1862: On board the steamer "Southwestern" en route to the Battle of Shiloh]

Since I last wrote I was quite sick for two days with the sick headache, but I am middling well now. Rob[5] is well and stirring around in the mud, and I tell you that there is plenty of that here this morning. [Nov. 17, 1862: Camp near Grand Junction, Tenn.]

---

5. Robert Ingersoll, Parvin's best friend in the army.

I was a-cutting down cane to get a place to lay down on and my knife slipped through a cane stalk and went into my leg, cutting a deep gash in the calf of my leg. But it does not hurt me much—only when I try to walk, and then it hurts me middling bad.

And the next day after I cut my leg, I had the sick headache pretty bad, but now I am well again with the exception of my leg, and I do not think that is a-going to bother me much. I hope not, at least, for I hate very much to be laid up at such a time as this—at a time when I am needed in the service of my country. [June 7, 1863: Camp near Vicksburg, Miss.]

———

Since I last wrote I have had a spell of the sick headache, and that is the reason that I did not write sooner. I wanted to get over that before I attempted to write, for you know that always leaves me with the big head for two or three days. And I have only just got over it now, and in fact my head feels a little dizzy yet, but that will wear off in a day or two.

Sarah, when I am sick is the time that I miss those kind attentions that you used to pay to me. You are on my mind nearly all the time and especially when I am not well. And lately I have been bothered a good deal with the rheumatism in my right hip, but still I manage to do my duty. And there is but few that know anything about it. [Dec. 24, 1863: Vicksburg, Miss.]

———

I again set down to try to write you a few lines so that you may know that I am yet alive and knocking around. I cannot say that I am real well this summer for I have the sick headache a good deal this summer, and there is something the matter with my legs. They are broken out with sores and I cannot get them well. And they hurt me when I have to walk, and we have a good deal of marching to do this summer. [July 14, 1864: Atlanta campaign near the Chattahoochee River]

———

Yesterday I had another spell of the sick headache, and I am not entirely well today. But I am a great deal better than I was yesterday, and I think that I shall get along this time. But I tell you that I think of home when I am sick and wish that I could be there. But such a pleasure at the present time is not for me to enjoy, but I hope that the time is not far off. [Aug. 6, 1864: Atlanta campaign]

b. Pneumonia [Lung Fever] and Respiratory Illness

During his first winter in the army in 1861, Parvin suffered a serious bout of near-pneumonia that laid him up for several days. He also suffered to some extent from other respiratory illnesses.

On that night [Feb. 12, 1862] I was taken with a chill and I kept having chills on the outside and a fever on the inside for the next two days. And then the chill left me, and directly after that the fever in a great measure left but it has made me very sore. And I am not well yet but better. I have been threatened with the lung fever [pneumonia], but I think that I am getting it very nearly worn out. I have not eaten a mouthful of anything for over eighty-five hours, but I begin to feel as if I could eat a little today.

I did not know how good the boys were until I got sick, and then I found that they were nearly willing to do all they can for me. A great number of them, that had better beds than I had, offered to give them up to me. And I concluded last night to go upstairs and get out of the noise a little. And one of the boys is a-making chicken broth today and he said that I was considered in. I cannot help but feel thankful to them for their kindness to me. And if I should get down sick, I think that I should be very well taken care of, as well as could be expected under the circumstances. You will see that I do not write very well today, but it is very hard work for me to write at all. [Feb. 12–16, 1862: California, Mo.]

I take this opportunity to write you a short letter, thinking from what I wrote in my last that you might be a little uneasy about my health. Well after I wrote I was taken worse and had to send for the doctor. He came and saw me and gave me some medicine and put a mustard plaster on my breast. And he told me that I was threatened with the lung fever [pneumonia] and that I should have to go to the hospital.

I persuaded him to let me stay until morning, and if I was not better, I would go then. He consented and he talked very kindly to me which made me change my opinions in regard to him very much.

And next morning I was better and I have been a-getting better slowly ever since. And now I begin to feel middling well again, but my eyes troubles me considerable yet. They are weak from cold, but I think now that if I have a chance I will get along. [Feb. 21, 1862: California, Mo.]

I am a good deal better than I was when I wrote the last time, but I am not entirely well yet. But I have reported myself fit for duty, but for some cause I have not been put on duty yet. I suppose that I will come on tomorrow. I shall have to be thankful for a good constitution and a strong will that I have not had a severe spell of sickness this time. * * *

You want to know if I am fat. When we left Jefferson City, I weighed 156 lbs., but I am poor now. I have not been lousy yet, but I guess that I can get a few about the time that I am a-coming home so that you can get to see some of them. [Feb. 26, 1862: California, Mo.]

We suffered a good deal from the cold since we left Corinth, for we had nothing, only what we carried on our back, and we had to carry three days grub besides. And you may be sure that we could not carry much clothing, but the most of us had a half blanket. But that was not enough for the nights were very cold and frosty and sleeping so cold and losing so much sleep made me almost sick. But I am well again now with the exception of a bad cold, and I am a-getting better of that. So I think in a day or two I shall be all right again. [Nov. 11, 1862: Camp near Grand Junction, Tenn.]

c. Smallpox, Measles, and Mumps

The dread disease of smallpox stalked Parvin's camps—along with other disabling diseases like measles and mumps. Parvin, however, never suffered from these diseases.

The smallpox is in the camp. There was a man taken with it in our quarters yesterday. Some of the boys feel uneasy about it. And all that have not been vaccinated are being vaccinated. Somehow I do not feel uneasy about it. [Dec. 2, 1861: Benton Barracks, St. Louis, Mo.]

Fosset[6] has been poorly ever since we left Jefferson city, but he is a-getting better now. There are a good many of the boys complaining now. We have the small pox, measles and mumps right here amongst us. [Feb. 26, 1862: California, Mo.]

———————

Sarah, in my last I spoke about sending you a bundle but I did not send it. And I shall not send it now for we have the smallpox in our regiment, and I shall not send anything home that might cause the spread of that disease. There has been only one case of the smallpox in our regiment as yet that I know of, but that was in our company. John Tillard[7] has got it, but I believe that he is a-getting over it now. [March 8, 1863: Lake Providence, La., above Vicksburg, Miss.]

d. Malaria

Parvin had one attack of what was probably malarial fever while working under the hot sun removing tree stumps.

When I last wrote I did not say anything about my being unwell, nor was I really unwell, but yet I was not exactly right. Our work for the last two or three weeks has been grading, and we have had an awful lot of stumps to dig up. And on the Friday before I wrote last, I was at work at digging up a large stump and it stood pretty close to the building. And the sun shone dreadful hot, and as I was between the stump and building, I was in a doubly-hot place, and I worked middling hard and I got overheated and I had to give the stump up for that day. But I sat down in the shade a little while, and went to work again at spading in another place a little further from the building, where the heat from the sun was not reflected quite so strong, and there I stood it until night.

———————

6. Parvin may have been referring to James M. Fosset, age 21, Company E, Eleventh Iowa Regiment. He was a resident of Inland, Iowa. He enlisted in the army as a sixth corporal on September 26, 1861, and was discharged on October 17, 1862, for an undisclosed disability. Roster & Record, 11th Reg. at 321.

7. John M. Tillard, age 22, was a resident of Muscatine. He enlisted in the army as a private on November 22, 1861. He mustered out of the army upon expiration of his term of service on December 17, 1864. Roster & Record, 11th Reg. 393; C.W. Soldrs. & Sailrs. ["John Tillard" search].

And the next day I worked but I did not feel really well that day. And the next day was Sunday, the day that I wrote, and I felt pretty well that day, and I thought that I should be all right again in a day or two.

But the next day I took the ague.[8] Oh! the dreadfulest ague that I ever had, and the fever would almost drive me crazy, and I have had it every day this week until today, and I have not had it today yet. This ague was brought on by that overheat, and it is harder to cure than the common ague, or I should of had it stopped two or three days ago.

But I have got some medicine now that I think will stop it, and it ain't quinine either. I could get plenty of quinine for nothing, but I did not want it. And so I let the doctors alone, and calculate to do so as far as I can. But if I am sick much in the army, it will cost me a good deal of money, for everything is so very high in the army.

Sunday Aug. 17th. Well, I missed the ague yesterday and this morning. I feel very well. I hope that I shall continue to do so. [Aug. 16–17, 1862: Corinth, Miss.]

e. General Illnesses and State of Health

The following is Parvin's general assessment of the health of his company at various times during his army service. In particular, he notes the names of his comrades who died because of various diseases.

You want me to tell you how many is sick in our company and who they are. I do not know how many there are nor who they are, but I think there are seven or eight but I cannot call their names. One has died, a man by the name of Hawk.[9] [Jan. 7, 1862: California, Mo.]

There is only one man in our company now that reports himself on the sick list, and he is able to eat twice as much as any man had ought to. But there are several that have not got stout yet, but all seem to be

---

8. Ague is a medical term no longer in general use. It is defined as "[a]n acute fever, ... esp. [a] malarial fever with cold, hot and sweating stages, ... [a]ny shivering fit." 1 The New Shorter Oxford English Dictionary 43 (1993 ed.).

9. George W. Hawk, age 19, was a resident of Muscatine. He enlisted in the army as a private on September 22, 1861. He died of measles at Jefferson City, Missouri, on January 4, 1862. Roster & Record, 11th Reg. 335; C.W. Soldrs. & Sailrs. ["George Hawk" search].

getting well. And that sick man looks well enough, but as I am not a doctor I had not ought to judge. But you know that it is my disposition to judge some things from evidence that I have. [June 5, 1862: near Corinth, Miss.]

I am well now and getting fat. I weigh 149 pounds and that is as much as I ever weigh in the summertime, and I think that I shall be able to stand this climate first-rate. There is but little sickness now in the Eleventh Regiment, and only one in our company and that is Tailer,[10] and I think that he will die if he cannot get to come home pretty soon. But it seems almost impossible for a private to get a furlough. There is great injustice done to soldiers in this respect as well as a great many other respects. Their lives are not counted of much value, and their feelings are not counted at all by a great many of the officers. [June 26, 1862: Corinth, Miss.]

I have very good health here, with the exception of a breaking out; something like the poison vine makes on me. I sometimes think that it is a slight touch of the scurvy that ails me, but it does not hurt me but very little. But it itches dreadful. I think that my blood is not in very good condition. I have not shaved off my whiskers yet, nor I ain't lousy as I know of, but that is something that I cannot speak positive about whilst I am in the army. [July 27, 1862: Corinth, Miss.]

I was sorry to find so many of the boys unwell, and two from our company had died since I left. They were sick but a short time. Their names were Small[11] and Web.[12] And there are a good many sick now

---

10. See Section 3f, infra, of this work for the ultimate fate of Daniel Taylor.

11. Isaac L. Small, age 19, was a resident of Muscatine. He enlisted in the army as a private on September 21, 1861. He died near Vicksburg, Mississippi, on August 15, 1863. Roster & Record, 11th Reg. at 387; C.W. Soldrs. & Sailrs. ["Isaac Small" search].

12. Parvin may have been referring to Silas Webb, who apparently was an infantry private attached to the Eleventh Iowa Regiment and who died at some undisclosed time during his service. C.W. Soldrs. & Sailrs. ["Silas Webb" search]; Ia.Gen.Wb.Prj. [Muscatine County] Iowa Civil War Rosters: Casualty List for Muscatine County, "Eleventh Infantry." He is not listed, however, among the soldiers attached to the Eleventh Iowa Regiment in the

and some are bad sick, and others only slightly. This is a very sickly place. [Sept. 12, 1863: Vicksburg, Miss.]

I am so dreadful tired of soldiering, where I am deprived of my liberty and denied all the luxuries and sometimes almost all the necessaries of life. That is one great reason why so many of us volunteers die off. If there was more care taken in providing the soldiers with comforts, there would be far less sickness and a less number of deaths in the army. But the life of a solder is considered of but very little importance. [Oct. 28, 1862: Camp near Corinth, Miss.]

Since I last wrote, another man from Co. H has gone to his long home. His name was Resipher.[13] He was a stout, hearty boy. [Sept. 20, 1863: Vicksburg, Miss.]

The health of the boys is a good deal better than it was a while back. [Nov. 8, 1863: Vicksburg, Miss.]

f. Army Medical Services

The medical services in the army were generally inadequate, given the poor state of medical science in the nineteenth century. And Parvin was acutely aware of this.

Oh! how tired I am of the soldier's life. I have been sick two days since the fight [Battle of Shiloh]. And if I have to serve out my three years, I am satisfied that I shall not be able to stand it even if I should escape the enemies bullets. * * * I have been sick more since I have been a soldier than I was in all my life before put together. [April 14, 1862: Pittsburg Landing, Tenn.]

Official Roster and Record of Iowa Soldiers in the War of the Rebellion (1908), and so the details of his service are unknown.

13. Andrew H. Rancifer, age 18, was a resident of Muscatine. He enlisted in the army as a private on October 7, 1861, and later died apparently of some illness in Memphis, Tennessee, on September 7, 1863. He is buried in Mississippi River National Cemetery, Memphis, Tennessee. Roster & Record, 11th Reg. at 377.

Oh! What a dreadful thing it is to be sick in the army. A man has no conveniences and but very little care. But such is soldiering. I am far from being well, but I am so as to be able to be around, and I have got to stand my regular guard and that hurts me to be up all night and lay out-of-doors on the wet ground. And the life of a soldier hurts me from beginning to end. But I suppose that I shall have to try to stand it a while yet if I can, and I suppose that I can if I do not get down sick. And I hope and trust that I shall not get any worse, but better. [May 4, 1862: Buena Vista, Miss.]

Daniel Tailor is sick and he has been trying to get a furlough but he cannot, and if he does not get one pretty soon he is a-going to die.[14] Our doctor is a poor excuse for a doctor. He has in more than one instance marked men fit for duty in the morning and before night they would be dead. That proves to me that he does not know anything about the human system. It is not the doctor that tended on me when I was sick; that doctor knew something. He is here, but he is not head doctor and consequently has nothing to say here. I wish that he was head doctor. It would be a great deal better for the poor sick boys, for he is a man with some feeling and those that he could not cure here he would send home and let them get well there. That business all lays with the doctor, and if he is a mean man, the sick soldier cannot expect many favors from that source. And there is not many of the boys that receive many favors from our present doctor. I hope that I shall not get sick and come under his care. [June 14, 1862: near Corinth, Miss.]

Danl. Taylor is dead. He died last night. I have spoken about him in one or two letters before. I was satisfied that he would die if they did not send him home. And he has been trying every plan to get home,

---

14. Parvin was quite prescient here. Daniel Taylor, age 28, was a resident of West Liberty, Iowa. He enlisted in the army as a private on October 14, 1861. As Parvin feared, Taylor died in Corinth, Mississippi, on July 10, 1862—about a month after Parvin's letter was written predicting Taylor's death. Roster & Record, 11th Reg. at 393; C.W. Soldrs. & Sailrs. ["Daniel Taylor" search].

but they would not let him go. And now, poor fellow, he has got his
final discharge. If they had of let him gone home at the right time, I
think that he would of been well and hearty by this time. [July 17,
1862: Corinth, Miss.]

g. Robert Ingersoll

The following three letters relate to the health of Robert Ingersoll, a fellow
soldier from Muscatine, Iowa, and Parvin's best friend in the service.

Since Rob. [Ingersoll] has been sick, I have wrote so often that I have
nothing to write about. I have not seen Rob. for two days now, but I
have heard from him every day, and he thinks that he is a-getting better every day. But he is very low and it will take him some time to get
able to travel. And the fever has not entirely left him yet, and I think
that he cannot get well very fast as long as that stays with him. [Oct.
4, 1863: Vicksburg, Miss.]

_____

I have just been up to see Rob. He is a-getting better as fast as a man
can—well, to be as sick as he has been. He is so that he sets up some.
He says that he thinks it doubtful whether he can get to come home
as they have quit giving furloughs at the hospital where he is. [Oct. 9,
1863: Vicksburg, Miss.]

_____

I have just been down to see Rob. He is doing first-rate. But he is got
to doing his own writing again and he can speak for himself. [Oct.
25, 1863: Vicksburg, Miss.]

Section 4. Camp Assignments

Parvin was assigned a number of tasks while camped in various locations
during his army service. These letters recount many of those tasks.

a. Carpentry

Parvin was a cabinetmaker by trade and was particularly qualified to do
various carpentry work in the camp. He got extra pay for some of this work.

For three days past, I with several others of our company have been working at carpentry work. We have been tearing down our bunks and remodeling our room and building our bunks up again, and now we have got things fixed up real nice. [Dec. 6, 1861: Benton Barracks, St. Louis, Mo.]

The squad of carpenters that I am at work with are at work in the woods getting out square timber. And we have quite a quantity to get out yet, enough I guess to keep us to the middle of next month. And when that is done, I do not know what will be our next job. But I fear that they will send us back to our regiments, and I for one would nearly as leave go to the penitentiary if it was not for the disgrace. * * * I expect to get my extra pay at the end of this month, and if I do, that will help me some, for I expect to get one dollar per day extra from my soldier's pay. And if I get that, it will help right smart towards giving us a start—if they will only let me work my time out at carpenter work or any other kind of work that they pay extra pay for doing. [July 27, 1862: Corinth, Miss.]

Since I last wrote, we carpenters have been ordered to our regiments. And I tell you that I was sorry, for I would rather be there than here soldiering. But I cannot have my own way now. [Aug. 25, 1862: Camp near Bolivar, Tenn.]

b. Canal Digging

Parvin worked on building a canal between the Mississippi River and Lake Providence, Louisiana, just north of Vicksburg, Mississippi, as part of the campaign to take Vicksburg. The purpose of the canal was to allow Union steamships, with soldiers and supplies, to get south of Vicksburg without using the Mississippi River and thus avoid Vicksburg's big guns on the river. The plan was to run the steamships with soldiers through the canal and into the lake, through the rivers that flowed south out of the lake, and eventually join up with the Mississippi River south of Vicksburg. After that, the Union troops would then attack Vicksburg from the south or east. The project was eventually abandoned because the canal could not be constructed deep enough to accommodate the

Figure 17. Grant's Canal, Lake Providence, Louisiana

Courtesy of the editor.

Union steamers.[15] See Figure 17 for a commemorative marker in Lake Providence, Louisiana, to this failed canal project.

> We came here for the purpose of digging a canal from the [Mississippi] river to the Lake [Providence]. And then I believe that there is water connection with the Red River, and we expect in this way to get below Vicksburg, and whether that will do us any good or not remains to be seen. I understand that McPherson's army corps[16] is to accompany us in this expedition, but as yet there is only McCarthur's division here.[17] I suppose that the rest will be along by the time we get the canal done. I understand that the rebels are fortifying themselves about

---

15. See generally David F. Bastian, *Grant's Canal: The Union's Attempt to Bypass Vicksburg* (Burd Street Press) (1995); Groom at 243–46.

16. General James B. McPherson was assigned by General Grant to oversee the building of the canal between the Mississippi River and Lake Providence in Louisiana. W. Groom at 244.

17. General John McArthur commanded a division under General James B. McPherson during the Vicksburg campaign in the spring and summer of 1863, but apparently played no role in the effort to build the canal in question. David S. Heidler & Jeanne Heidler, "McArthur, John (1826–1906)," Encyclo. of Civil War 1269, 1270; W. Groom at 243–46.

fifteen miles below here. They seem determined to contend our passage down the Lakes, but if the route is favorable I do not think that they can stop us. But time will tell. [Feb. 11, 1863: Lake Providence, La., above Vicksburg, Miss.]

I again set down to let you know that I am well. Since I last wrote, there has nothing of importance transpired here. They are still at work on the canal. [Feb. 27, 1863: Lake Providence, La., above Vicksburg, Miss.]

Since I wrote, they have let the water into the canal, and it is running through nicely. But they have not let any boats through yet and I do not think that they intend to. But that I cannot tell. I think the intention is to flood the country so that it will not be to guard, and then our troops can go to some other place. I think that is the intention and I believe it will work for the water is spreading rapidly over the country now. And in a few days we shall have to get out of this and hunt for higher ground. [March 20, 1863: Lake Providence, La., near Vicksburg, Miss.]

c. Building Fortifications

Parvin's regiment would often build fortifications to prepare for or ward off a possible Confederate attack. In particular, Parvin and his regiment spent a great deal of time fortifying the town of Vicksburg after it fell to the Union in July 1863.

Since I last wrote we have done but little except build breastworks and do our camp duties which is pretty severe. The troops that are stopping around Corinth are fortifying this place on all sides, so that if they keep off a little longer we will have good breastworks to fight behind. And that will be some help to us in case that we are attacked. And we are expecting an attack here now every day. [Oct. 28, 1862: Camp near Corinth, Miss.]

The prospect is now that our division will go to Vicksburg to garrison the place. And I do not like that much for we will not have a very good chance in there to get green corn and peaches, and there is plenty of both here now. And you know that I am very fond of both, especially the corn. [July 5, 1863: Camp near Black River, Vicksburg, Miss.]

We are now fortifying Vicksburg so that we can hold it with a small force, and then the troops that are here now can be moved to some other place where they are needed. [Oct. 25, 1863: Vicksburg, Miss.]

I have no news to write about. Things around here goes on after the same old fashion. Our forces are fortifying this place so that I believe that ten thousand good soldiers will be able to hold it against almost any force that could be brought against it. And this working on the fortifications is what makes our duty so hard. But it is all in a soldier's lifetime, and so I shall have to let it go on. [Oct. 28, 1863: Vicksburg, Miss.]

Things about Vicksburg goes on about after the same old fashion. We are getting the fortifications nearly done. And what they will do with us when they are done, time will tell. I am sure that I cannot. But I guess that there is but little danger of their sending us home for the want of some place to send us to. [Nov. 14, 1863: Vicksburg, Miss.]

The things in this part of the country are about as they were when I last wrote, so that I have nothing new to write about at this time. We have got the fortifications around Vicksburg nearly done, so that our duty is middling easy now and so that we have plenty of time to write or read or do as we please. That is, provided we do not please to do anything contrary to orders, and orders are not very strict so that we are around when they want us. [Nov. 21, 1863: Vicksburg, Miss.]

d. Military Drilling

Parvin's company constantly engaged in military drills during their early training and later in preparation for upcoming battles.

We are drilling pretty much all the time. We are getting ready for some move I know not what, but I expect time will reveal. You have a better chance to know the war news than I have, and so I shall say nothing about it. I shall have to go and drill. [Nov. 26, 1861: Benton Barracks, St. Louis. Mo.]

As it is nearly time for company drill, I shall have to stop writing and go and drill. And I am a-getting so tired of drilling, but yet it is necessary I suppose in wartimes. [March 26, 1862: Pittsburg Landing, Tenn., before the Battle of Shiloh]

We are still at Pittsburg Landing and the general supposition is that we are a-waiting to get a good ready before we make an attack on the enemy. We are a-drilling every day. But this afternoon we have been moving our tents farther back so that we will have more room for battalion drill. [March 30–April 1, 1862: Pittsburg Landing, Tenn., before the Battle of Shiloh]

Since I commenced to write this, I have been called off three or four times to drill and to do other things that has to be done about the camp. The fact is I have a very poor chance to write and I will be called off in a few moments to drill again. But such is a soldier's life. [April 23–24, 1862: Pittsburg Landing, Tenn.]

Since I wrote they have set us to drilling again four hours each day and that takes about all the spare time that we have. So now we have hardly spare time enough to wash our clothes or to write a letter. But such is a soldier's life and it will have to be so, and I will try and stand it. But soldiering is not my favorite profession. [March 20, 1863: Lake Providence, La., above Vicksburg, Miss.]

e. Guard Duty

A routine part of camp life was guarding the camp at night against possible Confederate attack. Parvin recounts some hair-raising experiences during such duty involving other soldiers, including: guards being poisoned, a guard accidentally shooting off one of his fingers, and another being shot by a sniper. Parvin often did this duty, at times under terrible weather conditions.

Last Friday night there was some eight or ten of the guards poisoned by a woman who went around among the line of guards pretending to be their friends. And as it was a cold night, she gave them poisoned whiskey, and they drank it. Some two or three of them have died, (so I hear) and the rest are in a fair way to get well.

Saturday night I stood guard duty, but nothing of importance transpired. [Dec. 2, 1861: Benton Barracks, St. Louis, Mo.]

You remember in my last that I spoke about being on guard. Well, the next night after I was on guard, the guard that stood just where I did was shot by somebody, but fortunately the ball only hit his arm. I think that he could not of been on the lookout. Well, so goes this world. One man stands in a place of danger and is not hurt, and the next is perhaps cut off. It stands a person in hand to live as if they expected death all the time, for a person knoweth not the time of its coming and especially in times of war. [Dec. 6, 1861: Benton Barracks, St. Louis, Mo.]

Night before last one of the men of Company K shot one of his hands. He was on guard and got to fooling with his gun, and put his right hand over the muzzle, and let a stick of wood fall on the hammer, knocking the gun off and taking two fingers with it. There is so much carelessness in the army that it is a great wonder to me that there is not more accidents than there is. [Jan. 14, 1862: California, Mo.]

Yesterday and last night is the first that I have been on guard since I was sick. I have been quite much favored (in that respect by our officers) for which I feel thankful, and I have no need to complain of my usage since I have been a soldier. [March 30, April 1–3, 1862: Pittsburg Landing, Tenn.]

As I expected yesterday, I was on guard and a disagreeable time we had of it, for it rained nearly all night, and it was darker than a stack of black cats, and I got but very little sleep. And in consequence of the weather and the loss of sleep, I do not feel in very good spirits. Since I last wrote I was quite sick for two days with the sick headache, but I am middling well now. [Nov. 17 & 19, 1862: Camp near Grand Junction, Tenn.]

The other day I was on guard night before last and a terrible night. It rained hard and the wind blowed terribly. I thought that it would blow down every tent in the regiment, but we got off better than I expected, and today is a cold windy disagreeable day. [March 30, 1863: Lake Providence, La., near Vicksburg, Miss.]

f. Picket Duty

Closely related to guard duty was picket duty where soldiers were assigned to scout the area near the camp for any Confederate troops. Parvin preferred picket duty to staying in camp so long as there was no real danger around. This duty allowed him to get away from the dirt and smell of the camp, get some fresh air and walk around as he pleased. But it was very tiring duty when carried out at night.

When I wrote you on the 7th of this month, our regiment was on picket guard. And we were on picket guard last night and today, but that is an easy duty here where there is no enemy near—much easier than staying in camp. For when we are in camp, we have got to drill twice a day. And out here we do not drill, and we can stroll around as we like. And it is very pleasant to get away from the smell and dirt of the camp, and to get out into the woods where we can have some fresh air and a good shade and the privilege of walking around a little if we want to. [June 14, 1862: Near Corinth, Miss.]

Sarah, … I have but little time to write and but little to write about except what you will hear in the papers, and it is no use for me to write about that. But the news [i.e., the fall of Vicksburg] caused the Fourth of July to pass off quite pleasantly, considering that we were soldiers and on picket and in sight of the enemy. But we feared them not. [July 5, 1863: Vicksburg, Miss.]

Last night I was on picket. And it was a bitter cold night, and in consequence I got no sleep, and I feel sleepy today. [Jan. 6, 1864: Vicksburg, Miss.]

g. Clearing Land and Miscellaneous Chores

Our work for the last two or three weeks has been grading [road building], and we have had some awful stumps to dig up. [Aug. 16, 1862: Corinth, Miss.]

———————

Today is the Sabbath but it is not a day of rest to me for today I have got to wash my clothes and go to the regiment, and there is various other little jobs that I have got to do. And the boss is after me now to go to polishing. And as I am a soldier, I shall have to obey orders. And by the time that is done, it will be time that I was at work at my other jobs. [July 13, 1862: Corinth, Miss.]

Section 5. Army Food

Like dog soldiers in almost any war, Parvin at times found the army food almost inedible and longed for his wife's cooking. At other times, however, he thought the food was quite acceptable—even good.

Parvin,[18] you speak about the girls eating apples and cracking nuts. Well we have as many walnuts and hickory nuts as we want and there is lots of apples if a person is a mind to buy them. [Dec. 19, 1861: Jefferson City, Mo.]

———————

Well, I have just been to dinner. We had bread, meat and hominy soup a-plenty. [Nov. 26, 1861: Benton Barracks at St. Louis, Mo.]

———————

Our grub has been rather short for four or five days, and I feel rather wolfy this morning. And whether we will have a full breakfast or not I do not know. I will tell you after I get it, and I am in hopes that it will be pretty good.

Well, I have had my breakfast and enough such as it was. But if I had something of your cooking, I could eat a hearty meal yet. We had

———————

18. Parvin is referring to his young nephew William Parvin Freeman, the son of J.P. Freeman [Parvin's business associate] and Parvin's sister Lydia.

for breakfast a half a pint of beans and a slice of bread about as big as my hand. And that was all, except the dirt that was on my bread and mixed through my beans, and I tell you what, there was plenty of that. [Dec. 9, 1861: Jefferson City, Mo.]

The way we live is enough to make anybody sick. We have nothing but raw bacon, hard crackers and coffee. And the coffee I do without so that it makes my living pretty slim. I am a-getting so tired of bacon and crackers that I can hardly bear them. But I am hungry all the time, and I have to eat enough of them to keep soul and body together. It would be so nice to set down to the table with you and have all the vegetables that I could eat (say fried potatoes and onions). Don't you think that I would eat a good deal. If you don't, I do. [March 15, 1862: On board the steamer "South Western" en route to the Battle of Shiloh].

Well, it is about noon and if I do not go to camp I shall not get any dinner. And as I am well and hearty, I do not want to miss that if it is nothing but hard crackers and fat pork. So here goes to pack up and start for camp. Well, I have got in camp and had my dinner so that I feel first rate now. [June 5, 1862: Corinth, Miss.]

Our grub here now is very good. Plenty of light bread and plenty of good meat, sometimes fresh beef and sometimes hams and good ones too. [Aug. 25, 1862: Camp near Bolivar, Tenn.]

Since I last wrote, we have done some of the hardest marching that we have ever done. And they have kept us on short rations all the time since we left Clifton [Tenn.]. I do not understand it for I know that there is plenty, and we have passed through places where there were plenty of government stores, in fact more than they could well take care of. And yet they kept us on short rations. [June 8, 1864: Some unknown camp on the Atlanta campaign]

Since I last wrote they have moved the hospital from Marietta to this place and me along with the rest. And I tell you that I hated to move down here for it seemed like getting further away from home. But I am here now and I must try and make the best of it. And from present appearances that will not be very good for they do not give us near enough to eat. But when they get things fairly started, perhaps they will do better. I hope so at all events, for this thing of going hungry is not so very pleasant, at least that is my opinion. [Oct. 19, 1864: Atlanta, Ga. Hospital]

Section 6. Army Discipline and Orders

Parvin frequently chafed under what he saw as arbitrary army discipline. He hated being ordered around by martinets and even ominously indicated that some officers might be shot by their own men in battle.

The more I see of a soldier's life the worse I hate it. It is a regular humbug. Now if I could go and fight in defense of my Country, it would be a pleasure to me. But to be kept here to be ordered about by a senseless pimp, it is disgusting to me. I will not mention any names for I do not know what might happen. [Dec. 28–30, 1861: California, Mo.]

I have been busy all this morning scouring up my old musket and that is a job that I do not fancy. But I have it to do or else get punished. A man gets punished sometimes if he should happen to wear his hat instead of his cap, when there was no orders given.

If being in the army will not cure a man's patriotism (if there's any independence in him), I do not know what would. A man is nothing more than a piece of machinery to be used oftentimes by men for his inferiors. And if a man finds fault, he is put on extra duty or punished in some other way. I have learned to keep still and do as I am told, and I escape tolerable well. But sometimes it grinds my independence, and if I did not hope for a speedy peace, I do not know whether I should be able to stand it at all. [Dec. 28–30, 1861: California, Mo.]

Last Saturday the drum was beat for roll call and there was three or four of our boys more than a block from their quarters, and they were slapped into the guardhouse. One of the boys had been to the hospital to see his sick brother. Yet that was no excuse for him and he was put into the guardhouse for going to see his sick brother (a guard house is about the same as your calaboose). It is considered a disgrace to go to the guardhouse. Or in other words it is a disgrace to go and see a sick brother or friend.

I think that it is a disgrace to be under such officers as we are under, and *I would advise some of them, if ever we get into an action, to keep out of sight in the rear or they might be in danger of getting shot.* [Jan. 14, 1862: California, Mo.]

I am now a-going to tell you about a piece of injustice that has just happened here. Our Sergeant Major was promoted to a Lieutenant, and in his place Robert Ingersoll[19] was appointed to act until further orders. Now in order to make a permanent appointment, it was very necessary to have the Colonel's signature. And our Captain goes to Ingersoll and tells him that he would do all that he could for him, and on the strength of that Ingersoll let the matter rest. But when the appointment came, instead of its being to Ingersoll as it had ought to of been, it was to Liman Banks.[20] Now I say that was injustice to Ingersoll and my opinion is that Banks will have to thank his sister [reference unclear] for his good luck in being promoted, as I am thoroughly convinced that it was through our Captain's influence that he gained his situation, notwithstanding his promises to Ingersoll. Banks is a

---

19. Robert Ingersoll, age 25, was Parvin's best friend in the army. He was a resident of Muscatine and enlisted in the army as a fifth sergeant on October 12, 1861. He was promoted to second sergeant on October 1, 1862, and later to first sergeant on November 1, 1862. He mustered out of the army on October 14, 1864, upon completion of his term of service. Roster & Record, 11th Reg. at 337.

20. Lyman Banks, age 19, was a resident of Muscatine and enlisted in the army as a third corporal on September 25, 1861. He held this rank when the promotion issue arose as discussed in this letter. On February 1, 1862, Banks was promoted to sergeant major apparently in place of Robert Ingersoll as Parvin states. On June 5, 1863, Banks left the Iowa Eleventh Regiment and was appointed captain in the Eighth Louisiana Colored Volunteers. He mustered out of the army on January 5, 1866. Roster & Record, 11th Reg. at 297; U.S. Civil War Soldier Records and Profiles, Ancestry.com ["Lyman Banks" search].

very good man but there are other good [men], and I hate to see such injustice done to one as good or better than he is. But such is soldiering. [Feb. 12, 1862: California, Mo.]

Section 7. Washing Clothes and Bathing

Parvin had to wash his own clothes and bathe in nearby ponds and rivers when available. Sometimes he did so without soap. When water was not available, however, he went dirty, which was often.

I came down into the woods to a pond of water to wash myself and clothes. And I have got done, and my clothes are hanging on the bushes drying. And I am writing to you while they dry. [June 5, 1862: Camp near Corinth, Miss.]

Since I last wrote, this part of the army has done but very little but lay around camp and eat our grub. We have not even a good chance to keep ourselves clean, for we have to haul our water about five miles, and we are allowed only so much each day. And that is only enough to cook and drink. And they do not allow us to go outside our lines unless we have a pass, and it is a good deal of trouble to get one of them. So that it is very inconvenient for us to get out to wash our clothes or anything else. But as we are soldiers we have got to stand it, and we try and be as cheerful as we can. But I frequently see some pretty long faces. [October 21, 1862: Camp near Corinth, Miss.]

I will tell you that we have not been where we could draw soap for the last two weeks, and I will let you guess the rest. But you must not guess too bad for we can wash some without soap if we have a mind to, and some of us have done the best that we could under the circumstances. I shall be so glad when I can get home again, and have you do my washing and mending for me again. And I hope that time is not very far distant now. [June 1, 1863: Haines Bluff, Vicksburg, Miss.]

I have been down to the creek and done my washing. [Dec. 31, 1863: Vicksburg, Miss.]

Section 8. Living in Tents

Parvin often lived in tents during his army service. When it rained or was very cold, this existence was often miserable.

I got a good night's sleep last night and feel first rate this morning. We are all in tents. It is first that I have stayed in a tent since I started, and I do not like it as well as staying in a house. But I have got to put up with things as they are furnished to me. [Dec. 9–10, 1861: Jefferson City, Mo.]

———————

Rob.[21] is well and stirring around in the mud, and I tell you there is plenty of that here this morning. There is strong talk that we shall move our camp this morning. I hope that we will and get out of this mud hole, for we are camped now in a regular swamp. [Nov. 17–19, 1862: Grand Junction, Tenn.]

———————

The weather is clear and cold this morning, rather too cold to live in tents if we could help ourselves. But as soldiers, we have nothing to say or at least we have no right to complain. But this morning puts me in mind of more comfortable quarters that I have left to help fight the battles of our Country. [Jan. 15–16, 1863: Memphis, Tenn.]

———————

I again attempt to write you a few lines to let you know that I am well and trying to do the best I can under the circumstances. For it is raining now and has been for the last three or four days and nights. And our tent leaks and our things are pretty much all wet. But we are expecting a dry day some of these times so that we will have a chance to dry them. [Feb. 17, 1863: Lake Providence, La., above Vicksburg, Miss.]

———————

The weather is very fine here with the exception of a considerable rain, and that does not hurt us much now for we have a good dry tent to stay in. And on the whole we are tolerably comfortable as soldiers,

———————

21. Parvin is referring to his best friend in the army, Robert Ingersoll.

but still it is not like being at home. [March 8, 1863: Lake Providence, La., above Vicksburg, Miss.]

Section 9. Bible Reading and Reflections Thereon

Instead of playing cards in camp, Parvin wanted to read a Bible and had his wife send him one. He claims to have read most or all of the Bible, but apparently was a bit of a free thinker. He believed in God and honored the Golden Rule, but wasn't all that certain that the Bible always contained the word of God. He even thought that both sides in the Civil War could claim the Bible supported their cause because "there is nothing so mean or bad but what the Bible will justify." [June 14, 1862: Camp near Corinth, Miss.]

> Sarah, you remember that you wanted me to take your bible along with me. I have wished many times that I had of done it, and I could enjoy myself looking over it and reading passages that we have read together there. I would enjoy it much better than playing cards. And if it is not too much trouble to Siler,[22] I wish that you would send it to me by him if you have a mind to. I will try and take good care of it and bring it back with me again. [Jan. 7 & 9, 1862: California, Mo.]

> I have read the Bible and Testament through some three or four weeks ago, and I now turn and read it as the notion takes me. I have read it through carefully, and I have marked down various places. [June 7, 1862: near Corinth, Miss.]

> The rebels hold that they are a-fighting under the sanction of the Bible, and we claim that the Bible is on our side. And as far as the Bible is concerned, both are right, for there is nothing so mean or bad but what the Bible will justify. [June 14, 1862: near Corinth, Miss.]

22. The identity of this person is unknown, whether he be a civilian or a soldier. In particular, there is no soldier by that name or with a similar name in the Eleventh Iowa Regiment. Roster & Record, 11th Reg.; C.W. Soldrs. & Sailrs. ["Siler" & "Silver" searches].

Sarah, you say I must do God's commandments if we do right. Now I want to do right, and I wish that you would tell me what those commandments are. But you know my belief in the Bible and of course you will not refer me to that unless you first convince me that the Bible are his commandments. [June 26, 1862: Corinth, Miss.]

In this letter, Parvin sums up his religious outlook as living by the Golden Rule. Many religious people today might very well agree with this outlook.

Oh! how happy we might all be if we would only do to others as we would have others do to us. That is the Golden Rule by which happiness may be gained. That is the true religion. And I would not give anything for a man's religious professions if he does not practice the Golden Rule. And if he lives up to the rule without making any other professions, he is good enough for me. [Oct. 28, 1862: Camp near Corinth, Miss.]

For as Solomon says, contentment is happiness. So let us learn wisdom from the Bible. Sarah, I read the Bible a good deal and the more I read it, the stronger I become in my belief. Sarah, I suppose that you will think that I am a dreadful bad man, and maybe I am. But you know that I am not to blame for anything that I cannot help. And I cannot help believing the way that my judgment teaches me unless I am convinced to the contrary. [Feb. 17, 1863: Lake Providence, La., above Vicksburg, Miss.]

Section 10. Army Pay and Camp Expenses

Parvin's meager army pay was often delayed, sometimes for as long as four months. He tried religiously to send home as much of his pay as he could without depriving him of some change to pay for miscellaneous items. In particular, he had to pay the cook to prepare his food, the camp barber for a haircut, and, astonishingly, the army for certain medicine he received when sick.

This morning we received our two months pay, and I intend to send $25 home. * * *Our pay amounted to twenty six dollars to the man, and I thought that I would keep the dollar as I might need a little change. And we all have to pay the head cook twenty cents per month for cooking and overseeing the kitchen department. I have paid him for two months out of my dollar. * * * And I have had to pay 10cts to have my hair cut. I am tolerable saving but yet it takes considerable to keep even me. [Jan. 23, 1862: California, Mo.]

We have not yet received our pay yet and it may be some time yet before we get any pay, perhaps not until our two months are due. [March 26, 1862: Somewhere in Tenn., probably near Pittsburg Landing, Tenn.]

I was in hopes that before this that I could send home some money, but we have not been paid off yet. There is now almost four months pay due us. And when we will get our money I do not know, but I am in hopes before long for some of the boys begin to need some change very bad. I still have a little change left yet, but it is very little. But I think that I shall have enough to do me until we get our pay, for I think that we will get some of our pay before long now. [April 23–24, 1862: Pittsburg Landing, Tenn.]

Father, I am sorry that I cannot send you some money. But as soon as I get my pay, you shall have some. I may be able to do so in a few days and I might not for two months yet. [May 26, 1862: Corinth, Miss.]

I went out to the regiment yesterday for the purpose of signing the pay roll. We are expecting to get our pay tomorrow and I shall have to go out to the regiment today to make some arrangement to send some home. As I cannot be there to see to it, I shall have to get the captain or some of the boys to see to it for me. I can't spare more than twenty dollars this time. I expect that it will be sent to Weed the same as the last was, and I shall direct it to Josiah.[23] And Sarah if you need any, call on him and he will let you have it. [July 13, 1862: Corinth, Miss.]

---

23. Parvin is likely referring to his brother Josiah Parvin.

Today we received two month's pay and I shall send you $15.00. That is all that I can spare now, for I owe some. And I do not want to run as short of change, as I have been, for it is not very pleasant to be out entirely. [Jan. 15, 1863: Memphis, Tenn.]

———————

Our regiment is being paid this afternoon. We are getting four months pay, or, in other words, we are being paid up to the first of March. [April 7, 1863: Lake Providence, La., above Vicksburg, Miss.]

———————

Sarah, yesterday we were paid off, and I received four month's pay, so that I can send you fifty dollars. I intend to send it by express. I shall start it tomorrow if I have a chance to go to town. And if not tomorrow, as soon as I can. So you may look for it from the time that you get this. [Oct. 28, 1863: Vicksburg, Miss.]

———————

Since I wrote, we have been paid off and I intend to send you thirty dollars by Capt. Parmer[24] when he comes home. And I guess that he will start in a day or two. He is coming home on recruiting business. [Nov. 21, 1863: Vicksburg, Miss.]

———————

When Parvin was sick with malaria, he apparently had to pay for his medicine. Quinine was free, but he didn't want it for some undisclosed reason.

But I have got some medicine now that I think will stop it [malaria] and it ain't quinine either. I could get plenty of quinine for nothing, but I did not want it. And so I let the doctors alone, and calculate to

———————

24. Parvin was most likely referring to Alpheus Palmer [not Parmer], age 30, from Muscatine where, according to this letter, Palmer was returning to recruit infantry volunteers. He did not belong to Parvin's Eleventh Iowa Regiment; he belonged to the Sixteenth Iowa Regiment, Company C. He mustered into the army and was appointed captain on January 15, 1862. He was wounded in battle twice: hit in the head at Shiloh on April 6, 1862, and hit in the thigh at Iuka, Mississippi, on September 19, 1862. He recovered and mustered out of the army upon expiration of his term of service on January 24, 1865. Roster and Record of Iowa Soldiers in the War of the Rebellion, "Sixteenth Regiment Iowa Volunteer Infantry" 1163 (1908).

do so as far as I can. But if I am sick much in the army, it will cost me a good deal of money, for everything is so very high in the army. [Aug. 16, 1862: Corinth, Miss.]

Section 11. Camp Clothing and Supplies

Early on, Parvin and his regiment were supplied with clothing and blankets—not always to his liking.

> We are tolerably well-clothed, but our clothes are not as good as I expected they would be. And yesterday we got one blanket to every two men and they are poor things, but the boys grumble enough about them without my saying anything about them. But there is one thing sure and that is the government was imposed upon when they bought our clothing as there is none of it first rate. [Nov. 10, 1861: Camp McClellan, Davenport, Iowa]

> We are expecting to get the balance of our blankets today. As yet we have only received one blanket to every two men. It is astonishing to see the amount of clothing and provisions brought here for distribution, and this is only a small portion of the army. Surely Uncle Sam is a powerful fellow judging from the rise of his family and the amount of clothing and provisions he supplies us with. [Nov. 26, 1861: Benton Barracks, St. Louis, Mo.]

Section 12. Lice

Parvin and his comrades often had to fight off lice, which was a most troublesome condition of army life.

> Some of the boys have got very lousy. I don't think that I have got any yet, but I am expecting them every day. I can assure you that they will come as soon as I want them. [Nov. 26, 1861: Benton Barracks, St. Louis, Mo.]

> We have no enemy to fight here except our lice, and I tell you that there is plenty of them. It is next to impossible to get clear of them for

the woods is full of them caused by men getting them and then throwing away their lousy clothes in the woods. But still some of us keep fighting them, and I expect that we will continue to fight them until we conquer them. [June 5, 1862: Corinth, Miss.]

———————

Sarah, in your last, you ask me if I am lousy, and I hate to tell you, but I shall have to say yes (or tell a lie). [March 30, 1963: Lake Providence, La., above Vicksburg, Miss.]

Chapter 5

Miscellaneous Army Experiences and Other Matters

Section 1. Travel Experiences

Parvin and his regiment were usually transported by steamship and rail when covering long distances during his army service. Although they marched long distances as well, usually this mode of travel was confined to somewhat shorter distances. The letters that follow recount some of these travel experiences, together with Parvin's reflections on what he observed en route.

a. Travel from Davenport, Iowa to St. Louis, Missouri [November 1861]

On November 16, 1861, Parvin and his regiment traveled on the steamship "Jenny Whipple" down the Mississippi River from Davenport, Iowa, to St. Louis, Missouri, where he trained at Benton Barracks, a huge army facility. En route, they stopped briefly at Muscatine and Keokuk, Iowa.[1]

> After we left Muscatine, we ran to Keokuk and there we laid up five hours to cook.[2] We left Keokuk at about sunset, and then we ran until about one o'clock Monday morning. And then we were caught in a fog and had to lay by until about noon Monday. And then we started and ran until daylight Tuesday morning, and then the wind blew so that we laid up until noon, and then started again and got to St. Louis about sundown, and it rained. I should think it did.

---

1. Roster & Record, Hist. Skch. at 275.

2. In this letter, Parvin uses the terms "ran" and "laid" in their nautical sense. The word "run" or "ran" is defined, inter alia, as "to sail before the wind." Random House Webster's College Dictionary at 1176, def. no. 32 (Random House) (1995). The word "lay" or "laid" is defined, inter alia, as "*Naut.* to take up a specific position, direction etc.: *to lay close to the wind.*" Random House Webster's College Dictionary at 768, def. no. 37.

And we started for the barracks about six miles off and it rained and was muddy and it got dark when we were about halfway out, and of all the slippery, muddy roads that ever I passed over, that was the worst. But we got through and we were a pretty looking mess, soaking wet and covered with mud. A good many of the boys fell down and they were mud all over, and those of us that were more fortunate were only muddy half way up. And take us all together, we were a sorry looking set. [November 20, 1861: Benton Barracks, St. Louis, Mo.]

b. Travel from St. Louis, Missouri, to Jefferson City, Missouri [December 1861]

On December 9, 1861, Parvin's regiment left St. Louis by rail for Jefferson City, Missouri, where they were encamped for a few weeks.[3]

You will see by the direction that I am at the capitol of Missouri and am well but I need sleep. We were ordered to march the next morning after I wrote to you. At five o'clock in the morning, we walked down to the cars about four miles through the mud and carried all of our firings. And in order to get off at five o'clock, we had to be up nearly all that night. And the next night we were on the cars all night, so that I have not had more than three hours' sleep in the last two nights. * * *

We were traveling pretty much all day yesterday and last night, and the distance is only one hundred and fifty miles. So you can see that we traveled slow and we examined the road pretty well so that we might not have any accident. The most of the country that we passed through was rough, rocky and almost good for nothing with the exception of a few places. I would not live in any part of [this] country. I begin to think that I am pretty well satisfied with Iowa, or at least I think I shall be if ever I get there again. [Dec. 9, 1861: Jefferson City, Mo.]

c. Travel from St. Louis, Missouri to Pittsburg Landing, Tennessee [March 1862]

On March 12, 1862, the regiment left St. Louis by steamboat and proceeded down the Mississippi, Ohio, and Tennessee Rivers to Savannah, Tennessee,

---

3. Roster & Record, Hist. Skch. at 275.

near Pittsburg Landing, where the historic battle of Shiloh was later fought [April 6–7, 1862].[4]

We did not run last night and the consequence is that we are not to Cairo [Ill.] yet. But we started early this morning and it is about noon now, so that we are a-getting pretty nearly there. And I have got to do all the writing that I am a-going to do before we get there, for when we get there it will be all excitement and confusion.

I have been on the top of the boat most all the morning looking for something to interest me. And we have passed some very pretty country and some very nice towns. And if I had of been a-traveling for pleasure, I could of seen many things to interest me.

But as it is, everything looks lonesome and deserted. As a man feels, so things look to him. I don't feel exactly deserted, but I feel lonesome. Yes, very lonesome, so very lonesome that I hardly notice anything that is passing around me.

I do not know anything about our destination yet any further than Cairo. The probability is that our boat will only land there a very few moments, and then we are off for some other place I know not where. And I suppose that it would not do for soldiers to know too much. [March 12, 1862: aboard some unknown boat en route to the Battle of Shiloh]

———————

When we left Cairo, we ran up the Ohio to the mouth of the Tennessee River and then we took up that, and we have came past the noted Ft. Henry.[5] And now we are a-laying at Savannah[6] (you will see where that is by tracing up the Tennessee River, and you will likewise see where Florence[7] is, our supposed destination). But they say that we have to fight our way from here to where we have got to go to.

———————

4. Roster & Record, Hist. Skch. at 276.

5. Ft. Henry was a Confederate garrison located on the Tennessee River just inside the Tennessee-Kentucky border. A month before, in February 1862, General Grant and his forces had overwhelmed both this fort and the nearby Ft. Donelson on the Cumberland River, making Grant famous for these victories and for his demand for unconditional surrender. J.M. McPherson at 396–402; B. Catton at 58.

6. Savannah, Tennessee, is located on the Tennessee River, slightly north of where the Battle of Shiloh soon took place on April 6–7, 1862. Savannah was General Grant's headquarters during this battle. J.M. McPherson at 407.

7. There is currently no Florence, Tennessee, in the immediate area of where Parvin was located. The town has since disappeared.

From the best that I can learn, there is from seventy to eighty steam-boats at or near this point all loaded with Union soldiers. So you see that we are middling strong, say from fifty to seventy-thousand men, a middling strong army, and I think if properly managed we ought to be able to accomplish something. I understand that we are under the command of General Grant. What our object here is I do not know, but I suppose our leaders know, and it is not necessary for us soldiers to know much about it. [March 15, 1862: On board the steamer "South Western" en route to the Battle of Shiloh]

d. March from Lafayette, Tennessee to Memphis, Tennessee [January 1863]

After the Shiloh Battle, Parvin and the mass of the Union forces slowly marched 20 miles southwest to Corinth, Mississippi. Parvin and his regiment were encamped at and around that location for the next five months. During that time, Parvin and his company were engaged in two military skirmishes at Bolivar/Jackson,Tennessee, and Ripley, Mississippi—located to the north-east and southeast, respectively, of Corinth.[8] Thereafter, for the next two months, he went out on expeditions looking for Confederate forces directly to the east at Grand Junction, Tennessee, and then to the south in Abbeyville, Mississippi, and Oxford, Mississippi. Finding none, Parvin and his company eventually returned to Memphis, Tennessee, on the Mississippi River.

All of these forays involved relatively short marches that Parvin does not describe in any great detail, save for the last leg—a two day march from Lafayette, Tennessee,[9] to Memphis, Tennessee.

> Since I last wrote, we have marched from Lafayette to this place. And we had a tolerable pleasant time; the roads were tolerably good. The first day we marched over twenty miles, and I had a big load to carry, and I think that I was never so tired in my life. But the next day I got along first-rate.

---

8. Parvin describes these skirmishes at Chapter 2, Sections 3a and 3b of this work.

9. There is currently no LaFayette, Tennessee, at the location Parvin describes; the town has since disappeared. At the time, however, it was a small town on the Wolf River, about 35 miles to the east of Memphis, Tennessee. Alexander G. Downing, *Downing's Civil War Diary* 90 (1916) (ed. Olynthus B. Clark). As an aside, Alexander G. Downing was assigned to Parvin's Eleventh Iowa Regiment, but to a different Company, Company E. He enlisted in August 1861, and re-enlisted as a veteran on January 1864. He was a fourth sergeant when he mustered out of the army in July 1865. Roster & Record, 11th Reg. at 312.

The same night that we got here it commenced raining, and it rained all that night and the next day. And last night it commenced snowing and it snowed all day today and it is snowing now. The snow is about a foot deep now, and the weather is very cold here. And I think that if they try to march us [in] such weather as this, there will be great suffering. But we must expect that whilst we are soldiering. We expect that they are a-going to take us to Vicksburg. [Jan. 15, 1863: Memphis, Tenn.]

e. Travel from Memphis, Tennessee to Vicksburg, Mississippi [January 1863]

Parvin describes a steamboat trip with his regiment from Memphis, Tennessee, down the Mississippi River to the Vicksburg, Mississippi vicinity. This transport was in preparation for the long campaign against the Confederate stronghold at Vicksburg, which eventually fell July 4, 1863.

When I last wrote to you, we were at Memphis. But the next day after I wrote, we were marched down to the steamboat landing through the snow and mud. And when there, we were kept standing there in the mud all day. And just at night we were marched on board the "Maria Denning" with two other regiments and a battery. And you may judge that we were some crowded. And our place was on the second deck in front of the chimneys with only one floor over us. And that night it commenced raining and rained all night, and the wind blew the water right in on us and the upper deck leaked very bad—so that we got wet and got our blankets wet, and we had a good time generally. And it has rained some every day since, but we have succeeded in getting ourselves and blankets dry.

Well, we had a very cold disagreeable passage down the river to this place. And now we are camped on the levee about eight or ten miles above Vicksburg on the Louisiana side or opposite the mouth of the Yazoo River. [Jan. 26, 1863: Camp near Vicksburg, Miss.]

f. Travel from Cairo, Illinois to Clifton, Tennessee [May 1864]

After re-enlisting for another three-year hitch as a veteran in January 1864, Parvin and his fellow re-enlisted veterans were given a 30-day furlough in early March 1864, to begin upon reaching Iowa. They were transported by steamship to Davenport, Iowa, from which they departed for their respective homes. On

April 22, 1864, they reassembled, along with many fresh recruits, and were transported by steamship down the Mississippi, Ohio and Tennessee Rivers to Clifton, Tennessee, in preparation for the historic Atlanta campaign.[10] In the following letter, Parvin describes the last leg of that trip from Cairo, Illinois.

> We left Cairo [Ill.] on the morning of the second on the steamer "John H. Dickie" and ran up the Ohio River as far as the mouth of the Tennessee River. And there we laid over two days. We heard that Forrest[11] was in the vicinity of Paducah [Ky.] and we were sent up in advance of the fleet to see about it. But we found it all a mistake about Forrest being in the vicinity, and then we stayed there until our boat went to Cairo and back. And then we got on board and started for this place, and we got here all right. There were thirteen boats in the fleet, two of which were gun boats. [May 9, 1864: Clifton, Tenn.]

g. March from Clifton, Tennessee to Atlanta, Georgia [May–August 1864]

From Clifton, Tennessee, Parvin and his regiment engaged in an extremely hard 300-mile march to Atlanta, Georgia, along which the historic Atlanta campaign was fought.

> Since I last wrote, we have marched over one hundred miles over a rough rocky country and my feet got very sore so that for the last two days I have walked with a good deal of pain. But I have managed to keep up this far. We got to this place about ten o'clock today, and I understand that we strike out for some place farther south tomorrow morning. I am in hopes that my feet will be better by that time. But as the time is so short, I cannot expect them to get entirely well, but I guess that I can stand it. [May 25, 1864: Huntsville, Ala.]

> Since I last wrote, we have done some of the hardest marching that we have ever done, and they have kept us on short rations all the time

---

10. Roster & Record, Hist. Skch. at 280–81.

11. Parvin was undoubtedly referring to General Nathan Bedford Forrest who was an outstanding Confederate cavalry leader. Bruce Catton, a premier Civil War historian, has described Forrest as "an untaught genius who had no military training and who never possessed an ounce of social status, but who was probably the best cavalry leader in the entire war." B. Catton at 151.

since we left Clifton. I do not understand it for I know that there is plenty. And we have passed through places where there were plenty of government stores, in fact more than they could well take care of, and yet they kept us on short rations.

Since I wrote, we have traveled about three hundred miles over a rough rocky country. This is the poorest part of the South that I have seen.

Well, they have got us now so that they cannot get us much farther unless the rebels give back, for they are only a short distance from us now. And they seem determined to contest every inch of ground, but I think that they will have to give back. But a great many of our men may have to fall. But that is what we are here for, and that is what we expect. Oh! this terrible war, what an amount of trouble it has cost already, and it is not over yet. But I hope its end is close at hand. [June 8, 1864: 11th Regiment camp on the way to Atlanta, Ga.]

Section 2. Camping on Southern Plantations and Foraging the Southern Countryside

Although he blew hot and cold about its justification, Parvin and his regiment would on occasion forage the southern countryside for food. They also camped once on a southern plantation—although Parvin had no qualms about this activity.

We are now staying on some rich planter's pale,[12] and I can assure you that we are not improving the appearance of it. But such is the fruits of war, and I do not pity them for they brought it on themselves. And I glory in their destruction. [May 4, 1863: in camp on somebody's plantation in La. near Vicksburg, Miss.]

Our grub here now is very good, plenty of light bread and plenty of good meat, sometimes fresh beef and sometimes hams and good ones too.

And the boys generally have plenty of vegetables, but Uncle Sam does not furnish us with them. But the boys draw them from the fields that

---

12. "Pale" is currently a little-used word in the context employed in this letter. It is defined as "an area or place enclosed by a fence; any enclosed area" or "a district within determined bounds." 2 The New Shorter English Oxford Dictionary 2075 (1993 ed.).

are handy. Somehow my haversack got full of roasting ears last night or rather this morning. Some things are very strange in this world. The haversacks of some of the boys that was with me got full of sweet potatoes, others of apples, some of peaches and some of various other things. It is strange to think how quick those things grew there, for how could they get there anyhow else. You may say that soldiers are hard cases, and maybe they are. But we are in a secessionist country now, and I think that they are in a great measure excusable for their draws on the vegetable orchards. [Aug. 25, 1862: Camp near Bolivar, Tenn.]

The last time that I wrote was at Abbeyville [Miss.], and soon after I wrote we started further south and we marched about ten miles south of Oxford [Miss.], supposing all the time that we were following the enemy of our country. But when we got down there, we found out that the enemy was in our rear and had cut off our communication and our supplies, so that we were put on half rations and then quarter. Then for two days our quartermaster gave us nothing, but still we didn't suffer for the want of anything to eat, for there was plenty in the country. And when the quartermaster failed to supply us, we went and took it ourselves. Such is the life of a soldier, and I detest it above all things that I ever done. [Jan. 6, 1863: LaFayette, Tenn.]

I have been out after peaches since I commenced this [letter], and now I have my haversack nearly full setting at my side. I wish that you had them for they are no rarity to me, for I nearly live on them and green corn, and the corn is not very plenty around here. So I hope that they will move us to some place where it is more plenty, and we will save the rebels the trouble of gathering it next fall. And you know that it is a shame to put them to any trouble of this kind if we can help it. [July 25, 1863: Big Black River, Vicksburg, Miss.]

George Bumgardner[13] found a bee tree the other day and six or seven of us went and helped him cut it. The tree was between eight and ten

13. George R. Bumgardner, age 21, lived in Muscatine. He enlisted in the army as a private on September 8, 1862, and mustered out on June 2, 1865. Roster & Record, 11th Reg. at 298; C.W. Soldrs. & Sailrs. ["George Bumgardner" search].

feet through at the butt. But we went to work at it with the intention to cut it down, and we did cut it down, and we got a nice lot of honey out of it and now we have honey. But it had to be divided into so many parts that there was not much for any of us. But we must try and find another before it is all gone. There are plenty of them down here, and we have two or three pretty good bee hunters in our company. [Dec. 15, 1863: Vicksburg, Miss.]

Section 3. Re-enlistment

On January 1, 1864, Parvin re-enlisted for three years in the army as a veteran. He was undecided on whether to do so until the very last minute. But when faced with the ultimate decision, he signed up again because he was totally convinced he had a patriotic duty to do so. The italicized portion of his January 6, 1864, letter announces his decision—which, no doubt, came as a bombshell back home.

His wife was appalled. She thought he was crazy. Parvin begged for her forgiveness, but stated over and again that he had re-enlisted because the country needed his services. He did say that the Army gave veteran soldiers a $402 bounty for their re-enlistment, but stated that this inducement was not the reason for his decision.

As it turned out, Parvin was almost killed in the Atlanta campaign on August 20, 1864, before his initial three-year enlistment had expired, and thereafter he saw no further action. Parvin's re-enlistment, therefore, did not expose him to any additional danger, as his wife had feared, and Parvin got a $402 bounty that the family sorely needed.

The following letters trace Parvin's thinking on the subject, leading to his re-enlistment—and ending with heartfelt apologies to his wife.

> I have not re-enlisted yet, and I think that I shall study on it a while yet before I do enlist. But if I was a young man (or what I mean is if I had not a good wife), I should not study long about it. But as it is, I do not think that I shall enlist again. But I make no rash promises for I love my country. And if she needs me, I had ought to serve her. But no more of this for the present. [Sept. 12, 1863: Vicksburg, Miss.]

> The office for recruiting veteran soldiers will be opened in our regiment in a day or two. And if I was a single man, I should be one of

the first to put down my name for I should then think it my duty to re-enlist again. [Dec. 2, 1863: Vicksburg, Miss.]

———————

Sarah, in your last you say that you think that the war will not last my time out. That is as much as to tell me that I had better join the veterans and get the $402 dollars bounty, is it not! I shall wait and see what you say, but the money is but little object to me. [Dec. 15, 1863: Vicksburg, Miss.]

———————

Quite a number of the 11th Iowa have re-enlisted in the veteran call, but I have not as yet. And I do not think that I shall unless you advise me to. I shall not for the sake of the money; I can assure you of that. [Dec. 24, 1863: Vicksburg, Miss.]

———————

Since I last wrote to you, there has been considerable transpired here that may interest you. *In the first place, the regiment has re-enlisted in the veteran service, that is over three-fourths of them, and I am now writing to you a veteran soldier.*

Now I do not want you to blame me too severe until you hear my reasons for doing so. In the first place, I enlisted to help put down this rebellion, and until that is done I have not accomplished my object. And in the second place, I did not like to see the regiment go home and leave me behind, and I thought ... that by the time that my present term expires, the fighting will be over. And besides, the government offers us a liberal bounty, and if I am killed that will help my family some. But I expect to come home in a month or two, and then I will explain to you more fully. * * *

Sarah, when I wrote to you a week ago, I little thought that today would find me a veteran. But I think that I have done my duty by so doing, and I do not think that you would want it thrown up to your children and mine that their father shrank from duty when his country wanted his services. But no more of this for the present. [Jan. 6, 1864: Vicksburg, Miss.]

———————

I do not think that I could be happy if I was to desert my country whilst she needs my services. I thought so when I re-enlisted, and Sarah I hope that you will not blame me too hard for doing what I considered my duty. [Jan. 31, 1864: Vicksburg, Miss.]

———————

Now Sarah, I do not know how to commence to write to you to give you the least pain for I would not say anything to hurt your feelings for anything in the world. Sarah, in some of your letters that you wrote after you heard of my re-enlisting, you write very short, and you accuse me of being crazy, and of my [not] deserving you and other things.

Now Sarah, I may be crazy and I may of done wrong to love my country so well as to be willing to deny myself of all the pleasures of the society of my family and friends. And I might of deceived you by holding out the idea to you that I would not re-enlist. But I was myself deceived for I did not think two days before I re-enlisted that it would of been possible for me to of gone in.

And Sarah, if I have done wrong, I pray that you will forgive me for I done as I thought was right. Sarah, I do not blame you for being worried about my going in as [a] veteran. It is enough to vex any woman that thinks anything of their men, and it makes me love you all the better. And if I have done wrong, I hope that you will forgive me. Sarah, I love no other woman as I love you, and I hope and pray that we may live long and happy together. [March 6, 1864: Vicksburg, Miss.]

Section 4. Recruitment for Navy Gunboat Service

Parvin and his regiment were solicited early on to join the Navy gunboat service. He and practically everyone else declined because of the exceptionally dangerous nature of such service and the claustrophobic conditions in the gunboats. His wife was relieved at this decision.[14]

There is quite an excitement among the boys today. Last night in the paper there was a call for volunteers in the gunboat service. And one

———————

14. Nonetheless, the Union Navy was quite successful in recruiting volunteers during the Civil War. There were 7,600 men in U.S. naval service in 1861, and 51,000 in 1865. Kenneth J. Blume, "Navy, U.S.A." 1398, Encyclo. of the Civil War 1398.

of the inducements held out is that they shall have their discharge in one year. But on considering the matter over, I concluded the chances for a man to get [out] alive was about one in ten. And to be penned up in a boat for a year if a man did not die, he would be good for nothing after that. So I have not yet urged the matter. And I do not know whether they would take me or not if I was willing. But I guess that I had better take my chances in the service that I am in. [Feb. 3, 1862: California, Mo.]

Sarah, you say that you do not want me to go on the gunboats. Well, I expect that it would not be a very good plan as I am not used to that way of living. [Feb. 21, 1861: California, Mo.]

Section 5. Army Duties Out of Camp

a. Guarding Railroad Cars

At times, Parvin and a part of his regiment were called upon to guard Union-controlled railroad lines against Confederate attack.

Last night I was on patrol guard. Or in other words, I with seven others had to go six miles on the railroad to see if all was right. And we took the handcar and when we started, there was not snow enough to do much hurt. But when we came back the car would not run, and so we had to push it nearly all the way. We started at nine o'clock and did not get back until after daylight, and of all the hard work that I ever done, I think that was the hardest that I ever done. And after I got my breakfast, I went to bed and slept until dinner was ready. [Jan. 14–15, 1862: California, Mo.]

In three or four days after I wrote, we were ordered on a march and we have been going nearly ever since. Our regiment went to guard a train of over two hundred wagons loaded with grub to Jackson. And then we had to guard the train back with a lot of secessionist prisoners. [July 17, 1863: Clinton, Miss.]

b. Unloading a Steamship

At Vicksburg, Mississippi, after the city had fallen, Parvin helped unload a steamship there. See Figure 18 for a photograph of steamships being unloaded by Union forces at Vicksburg in February 1864.

> Since I got back, we have been on duty nearly every day. We have been unloading a steamboat. But we have got that nearly done now, and I think that our duty will not be so hard now for a while. I hope not at least, but a soldier cannot tell. [Sept. 20, 1863: Vicksburg, Miss.]

Figure 18. Steamships Being Unloaded in Vicksburg after the Fall of the City

Courtesy of the Library of Congress, Civil War Collection.

Section 6. Furloughs

Parvin writes a fair amount home about possible furloughs in response to inquiries from his wife. For the most part, he was pessimistic about any immediate prospects. Gradually, however, he became more open to the idea.

Sarah, you ask me when I am a-coming home. That I cannot tell you for I do not know. But if I had a chance, I would come home tomorrow or even tonight if possible. But it may be a long time yet before I shall have a chance to see home. I will get a furlough sometime if I can. But I think that there are ninety-nine chances against my getting one to where there is one of my getting one. And if I was to come home, perhaps you would not know me, but my left ear is not shot off yet. [July 13, 1862: Corinth, Miss.]

Sarah, you speak about my getting a furlough this fall. Well, furloughs are played out, for they will not give any more furloughs, not even to the sick. So I expect you will have to get along without seeing me this fall. [Aug. 9, 1862: Corinth, Miss.]

Sarah, I should like to come home very well, but I shall have to get hurt a great deal worse than I was before they will let me come. And I do not want to be hurt if I can help it. But I expect to try and do my duty as a soldier, let the consequences be what they may. [Sept. 16, 1862: Camp near Corinth, Miss.]

I do not suppose we will stay here very long for they say that Vicksburg has got to be taken, and I suppose that we have got to help take it. And then they say that they are a- going to give us old soldiers furloughs. And I say bully for the furlough, for perhaps then I can get to see those I love so dear. [April 25, 1863: Somewhere near Vicksburg, Miss.]

Unexpectedly, Parvin was, in fact, given a short furlough. But not the way he wanted. Although not entirely clear from the letters, Parvin was (a) apparently wounded in an undisclosed manner sometime in the early August 1863, while serving in Vicksburg , (b) was hospitalized briefly at Marietta, Georgia, and (c) was then given a short furlough to Muscatine—as disclosed by the following two letters.

As can be seen, however, the relevant dates in these letters don't add up. Ostensibly, on August 31, 1863, he writes from a military hospital at Marietta, Georgia. Yet two days later, on September 2, 1863, he writes while aboard a steamer proceeding to Cairo, Illinois, en route to Vicksburg, after a short furlough in Muscatine—having left home at least six days before. It is likely that Parvin got the wrong date on his hospital letter, that it was written earlier than August 31, 1863, and that he was confused because of his injury.[15]

> I take this pen to try to let you know that I am not dead yet, and I think I shall be able to stand it through this time. I suppose that [unstated person] has told you the particulars about me being wounded, and I expect they have told you more than I can. And I am only writing now so that you can see that I can write. Yet it hurts me to write, and I shall write but little until I get better. * * * I should like dreadful well to be home with you, but I have got to wait until I am able to travel. [August 31, 1863 (probably much earlier): Marietta, Ga.]

> As I have been on the way to my regiment six days now, and I have yet to reach Cairo (I expect to mail this in Cairo) so I thought you might get uneasy if I didn't write before I got to my regiment. I might have stayed at home until Monday and of been further along than I am now, but I guess they won't kill me. [Sept. 2, 1863: On board the steamer "Hannibal"]

Finally, Parvin was given a substantial furlough in early March 1864—after he had re-enlisted as a veteran in January 1864. Indeed, all veterans like Parvin who re-enlisted in the Iowa Eleventh Regiment were given a 30-day furlough

---

15. This seems probable because the letter immediately prior to his hospital letter is dated almost a month earlier [July 25, 1863]. Parvin, however, tried to write letters home almost every week—sometimes more. His injury may have slowed him down a bit, but a month gap in the letters seems most unusual.

at that time.[16] Parvin eagerly anticipated this furlough, with his hopes rising and falling at intervals—as shown by the following letters.

> Sarah, since I last wrote, I received one letter from you dated Dec. 21. In that, you asked me several questions. But as I expect to be home soon, I will wait answering them until I get home. [Jan. 6, 1864: Vicksburg, Miss.]

> I told you in my last that I had joined the veterans and that I expected to come home soon. I do not know how soon, for we come home as a regiment and it takes a good while for so many to get started. But I think our prospect is pretty good to get off next month. But that is something I cannot tell. We may not get off until sometime next summer. [Jan. 15, 1864: Vicksburg, Miss.]

> There is a great deal of talk about when we shall come home, but it seems that nobody knows anything about it. But I think the prospect is good to come pretty soon, but that is only guesswork for the present. [Jan. 25, 1864: Vicksburg, Miss.]

> When I last wrote, I was in hopes we would come home pretty soon. But there is an expedition leaving here and I expect that we have to go with it. What is the object of the expedition, I do not know, but I understand that it is a big one. And if that is the case, it will keep us from coming home for the present. [Jan. 31, 1864: Vicksburg Miss.]

As anticipated in the above letter, in February 1864, Parvin and his regiment participated in an expedition in which they drove Confederate forces from around Vicksburg directly east from the Big Black River through Meridian, Mississippi, near the Mississippi-Alabama state line. In a letter dated March 5, 1864, Parvin describes this battle, and then comments "I think now that we shall get to come [home] pretty soon." And he was right. Parvin and the veterans in his regiment were soon thereafter given a 30-day furlough.

---

16. Roster & Record, Hist. Skch. at 280–81.

After this furlough, Parvin writes two very short letters while en route to his next assignment in Clinton, Tennessee, in preparation for the historic Atlanta campaign. The first letter, dated April 23, 1864, from Davenport, Iowa, laments: "This is a dreadful dark gloomy day, and I feel as gloomy as the weather"—no doubt because of Parvin's recent separation from his beloved wife and family. The second letter, dated May 1, 1864, from Cairo, Illinois, echoes the same sentiment: "I cannot get over having the blues yet from having to leave my home." Not surprisingly, he had the post-furlough blues.

Section 7. Advice to Others About Joining the Army

When his brothers Josiah and William asked in their letters whether they should enlist in the army, Parvin's advice was not to volunteer, but to wait for the draft. In fact, he told Lt. George Magoon to stay away from Josiah and William when Magoon returned to Muscatine on a recruitment mission. Parvin also discouraged his friend and business associate J.P. Freeman from volunteering. His reasons for giving this advice are a bit vague. But it may very well be that he didn't want to expose his brothers and friend to the dangers of army service—dangers he was willing to subject himself to, but was reluctant to advise others to face.

> Josiah, in your letter of the 27th you ask my advice about enlisting or waiting for drafting. My advice is easily given and that is wait for drafting. And if you are drafted, then come. * * *
>
> William, I received your letter of the 28th in due time, and I see by that you have some notion of volunteering. And my advice to you in regard to that would be the same that I have given to Josiah. I think that is the best way of serving your country. You say that you think that there is more men needed to crush out this hellish rebellion. And that is so and they will get them too. But I think that the proper way to get them is to draft them and then it binds on all classes. [Aug. 9, 1862: Corinth, Miss.]

> Wm, in your last you ask my advice about your enlisting or waiting for the draft. Now I do not want to be considered as discouraging enlistment. I am far from that. I wish that the North was united in this matter and would turn out to a man and crush this thing at once. But as that is not the case, I would advise all that are loyal to wait for the

draft for that is bound to fetch the men now. And it will fetch some of those sneaks that would be a great deal better off in the army than they are up there running at large blabbing treason as they go. [Aug. 6, 1864: Camp in Atlanta campaign]

————————

Lieutenant Magoon[7] has gone home as a recruiting officer. Another piece of nonsense for we have now twice or three times as many soldiers in the field as they know what to do with them. The last thing that I told George was to not get any of my brothers. He looked a little sour at me but said nothing. [Feb. 12, 1862: California, Mo.]

Section 8. Potpourri

a. Flights of Fancy

On occasion, Parvin did some dreaming about what he wanted to do when the war was over. The first was to leave the country for someplace like Brazil; the second was to move to Mississippi and live and work among his former enemies. Both seem like flights of fancy—the dreams of a war-weary soldier.

Sarah, you ask me if I think that the war will last three years. That I don't know, but if it does, I want you to be ready to leave the country with me as soon as my time is up, for I think that will be the best thing that I can do. And I should like to know whether you are willing to go with me or not. I think that some place in Brazil will suit me. [Feb. 11, 1863: Lake Providence, La., above Vicksburg, Miss.]

————————

I think this is a good Country to live in—that is, as far as the climate is concerned. Sarah, how do you think that you would like to come down here to live when the war is over. I think that I could make a living down here. [Nov. 14, 1863: Vicksburg, Miss.]

————————

———————

17. George Magoon, age 35, was a resident of Muscatine. He was mustered into the army and appointed first lieutenant on October 18, 1861. He mustered out of the army on October 26, 1864, upon expiration of his term of service. Roster & Record, 11th Reg. at 362.

Figure 19. Photograph of the Priestley Home in
Canton, Mississippi, Built Around 1852

Courtesy of the editor.

One of the towns that particularly struck Parvin's fancy was Canton, Mississippi, a small town located a short distance northeast of Vicksburg. Parvin visited this town in early 1864, in the aftermath of the Vicksburg campaign. This town is still quite pretty and is often used by film makers in shooting movies today. See Figure 19 for a photograph taken in 2010 of one of the beautiful homes that stood in Canton during the Civil War. Parvin may very well have seen this home and others like it when he was in Canton.

> In our travels, we went over some of the best country that I ever saw.
> I think that I should like to live near Canton [Miss.]. That is one of
> the prettiest towns that I ever saw. [March 5, 1864: Vicksburg, Miss.]

On occasion, however, Parvin came out of the clouds and was a bit more realistic about where he would like to live after the war.

> Sarah, in my tramps I have seen some very nice country. There is some
> very nice country out in the neighborhood of Jackson [Miss.], but
> there is none of the country in the southern confederacy that I covet

to live on. (Iowa suits me better.) And if the southern people will come back into the Union and behave themselves, they can have their country for all that I care. And I will agree not to trouble them any more if they will only do right. [July 25, 1863: Big Black River, Vicksburg, Miss.]

b. Thoughts on Wife Sarah and Sons Fred and Charles

Parvin loved his wife Sarah dearly and missed her very much. The same was true of their son Fred.

Sarah, this is a lonesome world to me without you are with me. And I miss Fred Andy very much. Kiss him for me. [Nov. 26, 1861: Benton Barracks, St. Louis, Mo.]

Tell Parvin Freeman[18] that I got his letter and was glad that he wrote to me. He speaks about Fred's being a good baby. I expect that he is. I miss his company very much. But there is one whose company I miss a great deal more. On their account I wished that I was not a soldier. [Dec. 9–10, 1861: Jefferson City, Mo.]

You say that Smiths folks have been a-making sausage. (If I had a little taste, it would be good to me now.) You must watch Fred and keep him out of the sausage. [Dec. 2–3, 1861: Benton Barracks, St. Louis, Mo.]

You say that Fred is full of mischief. Oh! How I would like to see him and his mother. [Jan. 7, 1862: California, Mo.]

---

18. Parvin is answering a letter from his young nephew William Parvin Freeman, the son of J.P. Freeman [Parvin's business associate] and Parvin's sister Lydia. U.S. Census, Muscatine County, Iowa, Household of J.P. Freeman (Sept. 4, 1850). William Parvin Freeman, age 19, subsequently enlisted in the army as a private on January 28, 1864, and was later promoted to second corporal. He mustered out of the army on July 15, 1865. Roster & Record, 11th Reg. at 323; C.W. Soldrs. & Sailrs. ["William Parvin" search].

Sarah, you say that Fred is a spoiled boy. You must persuade him to outgrow that. I do not want him to be boss yet. [Jan. 14–15, 1862: California, Mo.]

Sarah, you say that Fred will not go to anyone unless they have whiskers. I am afraid then that he will not come to me when I come home with my whiskers off. If I should happen to do so, you will tell me whether you want me to or not. I should be glad to know. [Jan 23, 1862: California, Mo.]

Yes, Sarah, I know that and I believe I have one of the best women living, not only saving, but kind and prudent. [Feb. 3, 1862: California, Mo.]

On Saturday Fred will be a year old. How I should like to see him, but I want to see his mother worse. * * *

Aunt Sarah, I am glad that you think of me occasionally. You say Fred is a good boy. I am glad of it. I was afraid that he would get spoiled. [Feb. 26–28, 1862: California, Mo.]

You [Sarah] sent me a lock of Fred's hair and want to know my opinion about the color. Well, my opinion is that it might be very much the color of my whiskers, but maybe not. It is hard to tell anything about it until he gets older. [July 13, 1862: Corinth, Miss.]

Sarah, I often look at your likeness [photo], and it gives me pleasure to look on the features of the one I love the best. [Oct. 21, 1862: Camp near Corinth, Miss.]

I sometimes almost get discouraged and think that I shall not live through my term of enlistment. And at other times I think that I shall and not be much the worse. But time will tell, I am sure that I cannot. If it was not for those that I love most dear, it would make but little difference to me how soon my time would come. But as it is, I want to live for there is one that is dearer to me than my own life, and for her sake I want to live and for the sake of our boy.

But perhaps my training would not be good for him. But I would try and teach him to be an honest man "and to do unto others as he would have others do to him." And if he does that, he need have no fears of a hereafter at least as far as I am concerned. I have none— for a just God can deal in nothing but justice. * * *

Sarah, forgive my faults and love me still. I remain your loving husband. [Jan. 6, 1863: LaFayette, Tenn.]

There are two references in the letters to another son who was at the time unnamed and was born after Fred in 1864. [Parvin had access to Sarah during a furlough to Muscatine in 1863.] Sarah asked what she should name the child. Parvin had no preference, but stated it should be a single name, not a double one. The child was eventually named Charles, the great-grandfather of this book's editor—a man whom the editor knew as the latter was growing up.

Sarah, you want me to say what the baby shall be called. And now I will tell you a name and I have good reasons why I do not want anything added to the name that I shall give you. If I were there, I could explain to you. But as it is, I cannot so well. [June 8, 1864: 11th Regiment Camp during Atlanta campaign]

Sarah, you wanted me to send you another name for our little boy. Now it makes no difference to me what you name him, but I would rather that you would not give him a double name for I like single ones better. But do as you please about that. [July 30, 1864: 11th Regiment Camp near Atlanta, Ga.]

c. Thoughts on Robert Ingersoll—His Army Buddy

Parvin's best friend in the service was Robert Ingersoll from Muscatine, Iowa.

If you see Ida Parvin, tell her that I am very thankful for the letter she wrote to me, and I hope she will write often. And tell her that I think

Rob Ingersoll is one of the best fellows I ever knew.[19] [Nov. 26, 1861: Benton Barracks, St. Louis, Mo.]

––––––––––

Ida, my views and Rob's about religion and the Bible are not exactly alike, but I think none the less of him for that. We both stay in the same tent and get along first rate and frequently talk of home. And I believe that he wants to get home as bad as I do, and that is saying a good deal. [Feb. 3, 1863: Yazoo River mouth, near Vicksburg, Miss.]

d. Thoughts on Theodore S. Parvin

Theodore S. Parvin was one of the early pioneers and leading citizens in Iowa history. His uncle was William Parvin [Daniel J. Parvin's father], thereby making Theodore and Daniel first cousins.[20] There is one reference in the Parvin letters to Theodore S. Parvin, and it is an unflattering one. What the occasion was for this biting criticism, however, is unknown.

I am sorry that Theodore S. Parvin acted so mean with us. He is a man that makes a profession of Christianity, and if the devil does not get all such Christians, then he will be cheated out of his just dues. But I have no fears as to that point. [April 28, 1862: Pittsburg Landing, Tenn.]

––––––––––

19. Parvin was probably a cousin of Ida Parvin, the daughter of J.A. Parvin. Ia.Gen.Wb.Prj. [Muscatine County], History of Muscatine County, Iowa, Biographical, "J.A. Parvin" 638 (1879). Robert Ingersoll, age 25, was Parvin's best friend in the army. He was a resident of Muscatine and enlisted in the army as a fifth sergeant on October 12, 1861. He was promoted to second sergeant on October 1, 1862, and later to first sergeant on November 1, 1862. He mustered out of the army on October 14, 1864, upon completion of his term of service. Roster & Record, 11th Reg. at 337. During a furlough on July 29, 1862, Ingersoll married Ida Parvin. Ia.Gen.Wb.Proj. [Muscatine County] Iowa Marriage Index 1846–1875 ["Robert Ingersoll" search].

20. An early biography of Theodore S. Parvin describes the arrival of William Parvin [Daniel J. Parvin's father] and family in Bloomington [later named Muscatine], Iowa, on March 29, 1839, and refers to William Parvin as being Theodore's uncle. This would make Theodore's father [Josiah Parvin] and William Parvin brothers, and Theodore and Daniel first cousins. J.E. Morcombe at 12, 108.

e. Directing Financial Affairs at Home

Parvin had certain debts back home, was apparently collecting rent from a relative, and was willing to sell his farm for a price. The details, however, of each of these financial matters are not entirely clear from the letters.

I want Josiah[21] to write about our business affairs, as I feel some anxious about that. [Nov. 20, 1861: Benton Barracks, St. Louis, Mo.]

Josiah, you want me to direct you about our business. Now I want you to exercise your own judgment about it. If you can get it without suing them, it would suit me the best. But if you cannot, you had ought to have it on some terms. [Dec. 19, 1861: Jefferson City, Mo.]

Sarah, you spoke in a letter about Uncle John's having to take a horse in part pay for rent. You told him just right about my being satisfied if he done the best that he could. Now if he has received any money and you do not want it, I wish that you would tell him to give it to Josiah. And he will credit it on my note and keep an account of it.

And what to do with the horse I do no[t] know. I guess that you had better tell Uncle to do the best he can with it, and pay the money over as directed above. But I will leave it to you and him to say what is the best to do with it. But it would be useless to keep it with the expectation of my ever wanting to use him. [Dec. 28, 1861: California, Mo.]

Last night I received a letter from Freeman stating that I might be held liable yet for the interest on that note that I took of John Smalley. If that should turn out to be the case, it will near about break us up. It will amount to about three hundred dollars, and if I have that to pay with what other debts I owe, it will take me a long time a-soldiering to make that much money. I wrote to Freeman about it last night, but it worried me a good deal. It bothered me too much for me to sleep, and today I am on guard, so that I have got but little time to write

---

21. Parvin is likely referring to his brother Josiah Parvin. Old Settlers Register at 130.

and I shall not get any sleep tonight. But these things pass off in a life-time. [Jan. 23–24, 1862: California, Mo.]

———————

Uncle John, you ask me what I will take for my farm. I will take $1800 dollars for all, o[r] $1700 for the farm without the timber. And he may take his own time to pay me inside of ten years if he will pay the interest yearly. I think that I had ought to have ten percent. But if I could not get that, I would take eight percent per annum. [May 26, 1862: Corinth, Miss.]

f. Photos of Parvin

No surviving photograph of Daniel J. Parvin exists, despite diligent efforts to find one in family albums and memorabilia. Daniel may have had one taken in his army uniform while in Vicksburg as that was his intention, but whether that was ever done is unknown.

Sarah, you say that you would like to have my likeness taken with my uniform on. I am sorry that I cannot get it for you. When a man is a soldier, he cannot do as he pleases. And now my clothes are soiled, and my hat is all bruised, and would not be fit to have a likeness taken in if I had a chance, and I have no chance. [Dec. 19, 1861: Jefferson City, Mo.]

———————

Since I wrote the sheet, I have been down to the creek and done my washing. And after I came back, I went down town and tried to get my likeness taken. But I found when there that they did not take pic-tures on Sundays. So I guess that I shall have time tomorrow at noon to go and get it taken, and then I can send it home in my next letter. [Dec. 31, 1863: Camp near Black River, Vicksburg, Miss.]

g. Prisoner Exchange

Parvin had certain reservations about prisoner exchanges during the war.

I sometimes think that those eastern men are too easily taken prison-ers. But maybe not, but it takes about all the prisoners that this west-ern army takes to exchange for our eastern prisoners. And that ain't quite right. But I do not blame the men. But there is a fault some place, and it is not my place to point it out. But I think that things will get to working right after while. I hope so at least. And when things gets to working right, the rebellion will soon play out. [July 5, 1863: Vicksburg, Miss.]

h. Promotion to Corporal

Although Parvin had been promoted from private to corporal by the time he was discharged from the Army in February 1865, there is no reference in the letters as to such a promotion. Parvin does state that he would like such a promotion, but that this prospect was unlikely unless he agreed to serve in a black regiment, something he knew his wife would not want—and probably not him as well.

Consequently, it is likely that Parvin got his promotion to corporal only after he received his near-fatal wounds in the Atlanta campaign, after his active service was over, and after the letters we have from him had ended. Here is what Parvin wrote on the subject just before the Atlanta campaign.

Sarah, you say that you want me to tell you when I get my commission. You need not be uneasy about that. You will hear of that as soon as it happens. But as I told you when I was home, that it would never happen, neither do I believe yet that it will ever happen—unless I should take one in a colored regiment, and that you do not want me to do. So I guess that you can calculate on my remaining a private to the end of my time of service. [May 9, 1864: Clifton, Tenn.]

Timeline of Pvt. Daniel J. Parvin's Civil War Service [1861–65]

Initial Training and Deployment Period
[September 1861–February 1862]

1861

Sept. 21	Parvin enlists in the Union Army at Muscatine, Iowa. Age 35.
Sept.–Oct.	Camp McClellan, Davenport, Iowa where Parvin's 11th Iowa Regiment was organized.
Nov. 10	1st letter
Nov. 16	Steamboat "Jennie Whipple" to Benton Barracks, St. Louis, Mo., where Parvin received basic training.
Dec. 9	Train to Jefferson City, Mo.
Dec. 19–20	March to Boonville, Mo. [prisoners captured: no shots fired].
Dec. 23	Train to California, Mo.

Deployment to the Battle of Shiloh
[March–April 1862]

1862

Back to St. Louis probably by train. Steamboat from St. Louis, south on the Miss. River to Cairo, Ill. Steamboat "South Eastern" from Cairo south to the Ohio River, east on the Ohio River to the mouth of the Tennessee River, and south on the Tennessee River to Savannah, Tenn.

Apr.   Pittsburg Landing, Tenn. [a short distance downstream on
                  the Tenn. River from Savannah, Tenn., probably transported
                  by steamboat].

Apr. 6–7   Battle of Shiloh [or Pittsburg Landing]. Gen. Ulysses S. Grant,
                  top Union commander. First major engagement of the Civil
                  War: approx. 23,500 total casualties, north and south. Parvin
                  in thick of battle, but not injured.

Corinth Mississippi Campaign and Aftermath
[April 1862–January 1863]

1862

Mid-Apr.–   March to Corinth, Miss. [20 miles south from Pittsburg
early June   Landing, Tenn.] Encamped at Corinth for approx. five months.

Late Aug.   Train transport to Jackson, Tenn. Train transports between
                  Jackson and Bolivar, Tenn. Train transport back to Corinth,
                  Miss.

                  Skirmish at Medon, Tenn. halfway between Jackson and Bo-
                  livar. [Parvin sustained minor injury: shot through the left
                  ear.]

Late Sept.   40-mile march to Ripley, Miss. and back to Corinth, Miss.

                  Two-day battle near Ripley. [Parvin served in reserve capacity.]

Early Nov.   Left Corinth permanently in search of rebel units, but found
                  none.

                  45-mile march to Grand Junction, Tenn.

                  40-mile march south to Abbeville, Miss. and then 10 miles
                  south to Oxford, Miss.

                  March to Lafayette, Tenn. [No longer a town.]

1863

Early Jan.   Two-day march from Lafayette, Tenn. to Memphis, Tenn.

The Vicksburg Campaign and Aftermath
[February 1863–March 1864]

1863

Late Jan.	Steamboat "Maria Denning" from Memphis, Tenn. south on the Mississippi River to near Vicksburg, Miss.
Feb.–July	Vicksburg Campaign. Gen. Ulysses S. Grant top Union commander. Parvin serves in reserve capacity in and around Vicksburg: no combat action.
Feb. 3	On the Mississippi River, opposite the mouth of the Yazoo River, near Vicksburg, Miss.
Feb. 11– Apr. 17	Lake Providence, La. [75 miles north of Vicksburg on the Mississippi River] Parvin helps in failed effort to build "Grant's Canal" between Mississippi River and Lake Providence.
Apr. 25	A cornfield 40 miles south of Lake Providence La.
May 14	Grand Gulf, Miss. [south of Vicksburg, Miss.]
June 1	Haines Bluff, Miss.
June 7–26	Camps near Vicksburg.
July 4	Vicksburg, Miss. falls to Union forces [same date as Union victory at Gettysburg]. Garrison duty protecting Vicksburg.
July 5	Big Black River, Miss. [directly northeast of Vicksburg].
July 17	Clinton, Miss. [directly east of Vicksburg].
July 25	Big Black River, Miss.
Early Aug.	Parvin wounded in unknown skirmish.
Aug.	Marietta, Ga. hospital. Short furlough to Muscatine.
Aug.-Sept.	Back to Davenport from Muscatine. Steamboat "Hannibal" from Davenport, Iowa, south on the Mississippi River to St. Louis, Mo., Cairo, Ill. ending at Vicksburg, Miss.
Sept.	Vicksburg [garrison duty].

1864

Feb.   Battle of Meridian, Miss. March from Vicksburg to Meridian near the Mississippi–Alabama border. Gen. William T. Sherman top Union commander. Only combat action seen by Parvin in Miss. Parvin not injured.

Mar.   Vicksburg [garrison duty].

Early Mar.   Transported from Vicksburg on steamboat "Continental" to Davenport, Iowa.

Mar.–Apr.   Veterans Furlough, 30 days.

The Atlanta Campaign and Aftermath
[May–October 1864]

1864

                Back to Davenport from Muscatine. Steamboat on the Mississippi River to Cairo, Ill. Steamboat "John Dickie" from Cairo, Ill., east on the Ohio River to the mouth of the Tennessee River, then south on the Tennessee River to Clifton, Tenn.

May–Sept.   Atlanta Campaign Gen. William T. Sherman top Union commander. Parvin sees extensive combat action.

May–Aug.   300-mile march from Clifton, Tenn. through Huntsville, Ala. to Atlanta, Ga. Heavy fighting from Huntsville to Atlanta.

Late June–   Battles of Kennesaw Mountain and Nickajack Creek, Ga.,
early July   northwest of Atlanta.

Aug. 20   Parvin seriously wounded outside Atlanta: jaw and teeth shot off.

Sept. 2   Atlanta falls to Union forces.

Sept. 6–   Marietta, Ga. hospital. Short distance north of Atlanta [un-
Oct. 15   known transport]. Parvin recuperates from near-fatal wound.

Oct. 19   Parvin transferred to Atlanta hospital [unknown transport]. Last letter. Long convalescence.

Home to Muscatine

1865

Feb. 25   Discharged from the Army. Returns to Muscatine.

1880

Feb. 24   Dies of cancer of the mouth related to his Atlanta war wound.
             Age 53. Buried in Greenwood Cemetery, Muscatine, Iowa.

Bibliography

Books

Allen, L.P., *The History of Clinton County, Iowa* (Western Historical Co.) (1879).

Bastian, David F., *Grant's Canal: The Union's Attempt to Bypass Vicksburg* (Burd Street Press) (1995).

Catton, Bruce, *The Civil War* (orig. published 1960) (Houghton Mifflin Co.) (paperback ed.) (1988).

Downing, Alexander G., *Downing's Civil War Diary* (Olynthus B. Clark ed.) (Historical Dept. of Iowa, Des Moines, Iowa) (1916).

Eicher, Daniel J., *The Longest Night: A Military History of the Civil War* (Simon & Schuster Paperbacks) (2001).

Foote, Shelby, *The Civil War, A Narrative: Red River to Appomatox* (Vintage Books, Div. of Random House) (paperback ed.) (1986).

Encyclopedia of the American Civil War: A Political, Social, and Military History (W.W. Norton & Co.) (David S. Heidler & Jeanne T. Heidler eds.) (2000).

Faust, Drew Gilpin, *This Republic of Suffering: Death and the American Civil War* (Alfred A. Knopf publisher) (2008).

Frank, Joseph Alan & Reeves, George A., *Seeing the Elephant: Raw Recruits and the Battle of Shiloh* (University of Illinois Press) (paperback ed.) (2003).

Grant, U.S., *Personal Memoirs of U.S. Grant* (original published 1885) (Barnes & Noble) (paperback ed.) (2003).

Gue, Benjamin F., *History of Iowa From the Earliest Times to the Beginning of the Twentieth Century*, Vol. IV Iowa Biography (The Century History Co., New York) (1903).

Groom, Winston, *Vicksburg 1863* (Vintage Civil War Library, Vintage Books, Div. of Random House, Inc. (paperback ed.) (2009).

History of Muscatine County Iowa From the Earliest Settlements to the Present Time, Vol. I (S.J. Clarke Publishing Co., Chicago) (Irving B. Richman, supervising ed.) (1911).

McPherson, James M., *Battle Cry of Freedom* (Oxford Univ. Press) (1988).

Morcombe, Joseph E., *The Life and Labors of Theodore Sutton Parvin A.M. LL.D.* (Allen Printing Co., Clinton, Ia.) (1908).

Oxford Companion to United States History (Paul S. Boyer ed.) (Oxford Univ. Press) (2001).

Phisterer, Frederick, *Statistical Record of the Armies of the United States* (Charles Scribners Sons) (1888).

Roster and Record of Iowa Soldiers in the War of the Rebellion, Vol. II, 9th–16th Regiments—Infantry (Des Moines, Ia.; Emory H. English, State Printer; E.D. Chassell, State Binder) (1908).

Sheehan-Dean, Aaron, *Concise Historical Atlas of the American Civil War* (Oxford University Press) (2009).

Walton, Josiah Proctor, *Pioneer Papers: comprising a collection of early events of Bloomington, Iowa, now Muscatine, and its surroundings, being a short history of the business men, the schools, the churches and the early politics of the pioneers* (Muscatine Daily Mail Publisher) (Lib. of Congress no. F629.M9 W18) (1899).

Web Sites

Civil War Soldiers and Sailors Website, National Park Service [n.ps.gov/c/wss/soldiers].

Greenwood Cemetery Records, Muscatine, Iowa [Ancestry.com].

Iowa Gen Web Project [iagenweb.org].

Muscatine County, Iowa, Register of Old Settlers, Book One, Iowa Gen Web Project [iagenweb.org].

Index

Note: *f* indicates figure; *n*, footnote.